WE ARE HERE TO HELP . . .
AND SO, WELCOME TO THE 12 IMPERATIVES OF THE **BIG LIE**

1. Accept that every time a consumer answers a question from you something strategically important—no matter how shallow or self-serving the answer—will be revealed.

2. Recognize that what consumers say out loud about their lives, their dreams, their needs... can be accurately and purposefully interpreted by only your company's smartest people.

3. Know that when a consumer is invited to express opinions and preferences (particularly online) he might well imagine that the stranger he is addressing is actually a version of himself—a better self, an ideal version.

4. Approach consumers as if you like them (because you genuinely do); for you want them to succeed in life and you do not think they are there to be manipulated even if they may occasionally dupe themselves.

5. Take strength and inspiration from the knowledge that your consumer will never be your friend.

6. Acknowledge that all moments of choice are social experiences to some measurable extent and that this connection to the wider cultural order carries a potent influence—of which the consumer may be personally unaware or privately reluctant to recognize.

7. Validate in your mind that the goal of all insight is to dissipate confusion and clear the way to better corporate decisions—a task made heavy but not impossible by the multiple ways in which consumers can talk to you in the modern era and by the multiple personalities they can inhabit.

8. Embrace paradox and let it energize creativity: insight has to address what consumers think they ought to say in public while servicing their private motives that can be hidden, muddled, contradictory.

9. Track the evolution of social norms (received wisdoms of our time, pressures to conform to certain standards or attitudes, all the prevailing ethics...) as if you were a space engineer tracking gravitational pull—for your brand requires science to meet creativity.

10. Dramatize in your mind the trends that are shaping your commercial prospects and put them under continuous re-scrutiny in order to keep your market plans and executions on an endless edge of change.

11. Recognize that brand-ownership can become an obsession: you, the owner, may think of nothing else except your product but out there your customer has a life to lead, an often messy life with which you must engage in full.

12. Use market research like a surgeon uses a scalpel but not like a racing driver uses a steering wheel—cutting through to the opportunity rather than racing around the circuit.

WHAT CLIENTS SAY ABOUT FUTURE FOUNDATION . . .

"More a partner than an agency, Future Foundation have been a fantastic trend experts resource for us. Not only do they provide the broad macroeconomic view, they also help us understand the important trends for our sector and their key manifestations—not just now but also how they will evolve in the future. Instrumental in developing our 2020 thinking, Future Foundation is a great partner, with sharp business acumen, great responsiveness and a genuine desire to help us understand the future".

Shruti Singh, Speedo

"We have worked with Future Foundation for over 10 years now. They are our first port of call for any external consumer related trends or external data. The insights they provide are highly relevant to our business and are continuously used to inform our thinking. We have worked closely with Future Foundation to apply their research findings to our own customer segmentation. They are a key insight partner".

Roy Hammond, Barclays

"Meabh and the team at Future Foundation have been the ideal partner to help us brew a vision for our category. FF possesses the blend of talents, the professionalism and the enthusiasm necessary to turn a mass of consumer information into a simple but compelling message engaging us for the future".

Yvan Goupil, SAB Miller

"British Airways has been very impressed with the quality of service we get from Future Foundation. We sincerely appreciate the responsiveness of the team and they work with the many stakeholders to guide them to find the rich veins of information that lies within **nVision**. We look forward to building on a great beginning with you for years to come".

Glenys Stokes, British Airways

"**nVision** provides invaluable support around both existing and emerging consumer trends, partnering with us on the challenge to decipher the often complex puzzle of the 'ever evolving consumer', and providing insights which inspire and fuel communications that resonate with the consumer across our clients' various categories and markets".

Peter Foster, OMD

THE BIG LIE

. . . or interpreting your global customer's
inner life for profit

Christophe Jouan
Meabh Quoirin
James Murphy

Future Foundation
www.futurefoundation.net

BALBOA.
PRESS

A DIVISION OF HAY HOUSE

Balboa Press books may be ordered through booksellers or by contacting:

Balboa Press
A Division of Hay House
1663 Liberty Drive
Bloomington, IN 47403
www.balboapress.com
1-(877) 407-4847

Printed in the United States of America.

ISBN: 978-1-4525-7890-3 (sc)
ISBN: 978-1-4525-7891-0 (e)

Library of Congress Control Number: 2013913755

A CIP catalog record for this book is available from the Library of Congress

Balboa Press rev. date: 08/20/2013

CONTENTS

WHERE THE STORY BEGINS . . .

Imagine this.

There is a man in San Francisco today who wants to buy a gift in celebration of his wife's thirtieth birthday. He sits down with a beer and concentrates. What would she *really* like? She told you not to bother with anything fancy but . . .

Now, let's think, what has she been given in previous years and during the last Holidays? Inadvertent but thoughtless duplication must be avoided. What kind of things, meanwhile, do her friends receive from their men? Should this year's present be something she can definitely parade in front of them? How important is that kind of vibe to her these days? Let's think this one through . . .

And what about the cost? Obviously, too great an outlay—a diamond, a vacation, new trainers—might create a dangerous precedent for birthdays to come. But this cannot be said, indeed barely thought, out loud.

Besides she told you recently that she had read an article about precious stones and the role they play in funding cruel wars in Africa—and so a diamond might be insensitive. And she does worry about big clothing companies not looking after their workers very well in the Far East. There was another such story in **The Huffington Post** last week.

Anyway, she is always saying that the family must budget better and she has been known to deprecate even sporadic over-indulgence.

(Remember when you brought home all those pints of **Ben & Jerry's** because they were on sale?). But, for this special birthday, does she secretly want the boat to be pushed out, *whatever she says*?

And when the big moment comes and the present is unwrapped, how to know just how successful the choice has been? A loving embrace? A squeal of joy? Or maybe just a troublesome Mona Lisa smile? Our man wrestles the same basic problem, what Sherlock Holmes used to call a three-pipe problem, every year . . . And it seems to get more complicated.

Even in the simplest workaday stories of family life, a parable for all that we are about to discuss might readily be found.

But let's leave Jack and Lisa for now and come back to them later.

In recent years, the business of accurately identifying the most potent social trends and predicting their evolution has got big, very big. This can be verified by the more elevated role insight professionals—as they are now regularly called—are invited to play inside the organizations behind big brands. And confirmed too by the wave of scholarly books tracing the forward trajectory of how we, consumer-citizens worldwide, shop and eat and have fun and talk to one another and, generally, try to draw contentment out of life.

More, the authority once held by conventional forecasts of the strictly economic kind now seems threadbare to the point of irreparably torn—the inevitable legacy of credit crunch, downturn, sovereign state indebtedness and all the sad vicissitudes of governmental policy-making across the Western world in recent years. The big numbers have just been wrong too often. So, where do we, those who need to plan, turn in search of the deepest truths about all our futures?

These days, the best people in business life, we humbly submit, appreciate this fundamental truth: if it's hard to be smart then it's getting harder. There is no one discipline, no single technique, no irreducible principle which will guide you to a perfect prediction of what your customers are going to want or need from you next—or in a decade from now.

Along the way, the process loosely known as globalization (the long-term transformative power of which is still perhaps being underestimated?) naturally drives new competitive disruptions into virtually every established commercial sector. And along that same way, the **Digital Revolution** has equipped consumers with what we might call seriously *effective knowledge*—just as the first wave of post-War democratized prosperity bestowed *effective demand* on millions of households.

There is another element here, a motion that just will not subside. Macro-economic volatility and the uncertainties surrounding personal income growth in both the USA and Europe have created a new and measurable *ruthlessness* among consumers. They will guard their living standards like upright members of the Corleone family. They will happily screw big brands just as any 20th century monopolistic supplier might once have tried to screw *them*.

There, you do not hear language like that in the **Harvard Business Review**, do you?

So where is this line of thinking taking us?

At Future Foundation, we carry out annual quantitative research programs in 24 countries across the world—from Sweden to South Africa, South Korea to Spain, Australia to the Americas. We do not need to wait for our clients to tell us what questions to put. In a sense, that is the easy part.

How are our consumer-citizens organizing their household budgets and savings?

Why are they using social media so much?

Are they more worried about their kids' futures than they were even a little while back?

What new measures, if any, are they taking to preserve personal health and well-being?

*What does the term **luxury** really mean to them now?*

If the planet is warming—then how much do they care and what are they doing about it as parents, as shoppers, as entrepreneurs?

And so on.

In addition, we run 200 trendspotters on the streets of more than 50 countries. They send living examples of trends at work in their communities which we analyze and collate. We also talk to hundreds of people in conventional qualitative exercises, digging for deluxe vox pops. At our Future Foundation HQ, we can work (ie able to read, able to talk, able to present) in twelve languages, from Mandarin to German. We could make no legitimate claim of being capable of interpreting global human reality without such a deliberately acquired asset within our human resources. And, frankly, we do not see how anyone could.

And while we are talking about the skill and talent requirements for any such endeavor, let's lay down one of the rarely spoken truths about global research. Crafting survey questions for consumer-citizens who eat/pray/love, *mutatis mutandis*, across five continents is positively algebraic in its complexity now. Even when the best, most creative people do it they will go through more questionnaire drafts than successful sitcom writers go through scripts. Nothing, moreover, is to be lost—or inadvertently, unwantedly gained—in translation. (Think, for instance, how punctilious one has to be in checking the translation of the word "happy" or "attractive" or phrases like "entertaining at home" into Spanish, Mandarin, German, Hindi . . .). Any question has to work in multicultural-digital not uniform-analog.

There is another variable too. We have to monitor just how differently people answer questions in measurable correlation *to the way in which they are asked*. For example, when questions are put face-to-face, consumer-citizens are often nicer, more ethically alert, more sensitive to the pain or the poverty of others than they are if they provide answers as they sit at home, alone in their kitchen perhaps, typing their answers into an inanimate box.

This precept drives the title of our book and energizes the essentialist proposition about human beings which follows here.

For now, the simple observation we make is this.

Global consumer research. Hell of a job.

This said, we set about coining insight-bearing and actionable trends, hearing whatever secret harmonies our research brings to life, bringing brands closer to the lives of those who buy their products now or might well, if sensitively invited, buy them tomorrow.

This is indeed our job. So far, so challenging. But, like any serious trends agency, we are gathering from year to year surging sierras of statistics, reams of print-out, multi-charted distributions of the opinions of thousands and thousands of people *and*, ineluctably, jagged piles of contradictory evidence and paradoxical attitudes, telling of a consumerism so contrarian that, beside it, quantum mechanics seems like rookie sudoku.

If you are in business at any level, then you will know what we mean here. Information, meant to liberate, can confuse and crush, cluttering the path to a good decision or a promising new initiative rather than clearing it. As she sets out to make her market projects sing for her, any leader in any consumer-facing business can easily get too much intel of the only partially useful kind. What does she really need to know, really need to *see*?

And those consumers—well, why is it that what they say is so often not what they do?

How come they say they care about something but do not buy the product that would really do the caring for them? Why is it that even when you know they are moved by a particular feeling or appetite it's still so difficult to establish by *how much*? And how do they, as they move from market-sector to market-sector and store to store and offline to online, actually sift the competing priorities swirling in their heads in order to alight on good (if not always objectively optimal) decisions? Why are they so damned *irrational* a lot of the time? Why do they sometimes seem to purposefully conspire in their own disillusionment?

Let's get back to Jack and Lisa. Just for a minute.

They want to buy a car. And they are, naturally, moved to buy American-built. And they are moved to buy green—as well as eco-friendly. And they are moved to buy serious fuel-economy. And they are moved to buy glamorous—but, obviously, super-safe too. And they are moved to buy new—but they feel financially compelled to buy second-hand. Also, they are quite interested in the car which, of all the options in their price range, will lose its re-sale value most slowly as the years pass. They like their old **Ford Fusion** but they have gotten a bit bored with it. But neither of them says this out loud to one another. In fact, very little of the above is openly discussed by the couple at all as the whole project is but moderately interesting to both of them. Lisa casually remarks that a lot of the other classroom moms are switching to **Zipcar**. But Jack insists: he has always had his own car, just like all the men in his family in living memory.

Anyway, not all of these considerations can, it is plain, be accommodated in the final choice of marque. Plain too, that some of them weigh more than others in the minds of our buyers—and weigh more or less as they variously scan autosale websites, talk to friends, listen to the salespeoples' pitch at the car dealerships they visit. The final decision will have crawled on a thousand feet before Jack, having changed his mind twice in the week before, drives that **Honda Fit** into the driveway of their Richmond home.

Now, a good question is: at what point was the decision in favor of a particular brand of hatchback really clinched? How much of the inner debate about the choice of car was *adjectival* and how much truly *central*? How much were Jack and Lisa going through a clichéd, slightly robotic list of what they thought they *ought* to consider and what were the factors—social, economic and psychological—genuinely shaping the ultimate buying moment? Did, for instance, their concerns for the eco impact of any one brand against another actually, in the end or even at the beginning, matter *at all*?

Before we continue, let us say that we appreciate that the contemporary and still emerging claims for Big Data bring something potentially subversive into this kind of discussion. Some are starting to argue that knowing the inner triggers of consumer choice matters less when an ever swelling wave of still accumulating data can reveal so much about the movements and decisions of millions of individuals—and *crucially* purify all the predictions about what those consumers will do next. Our attitude is that an understanding of causality—with special reference to any gap which may exist between private inclinations and social narratives—remains, *pace* Big Data, a vital element in developing brand strategy. Data scientists may accurately anticipate the spread of a flu epidemic up and down the East Coast. But why should victims visit *your* drug store, buy *your* palliative medications, take a rest cure in *your* resort, renew their health insurance with *your* company, start to improve their resistance to disease with *your* vitamin supplements and juices? Why indeed. There will be more on this dimension in the final section of the **Big Lie**.

Meanwhile, a pantechnicon of modern business books address, in their own often roundabout way, the issue of what motives drive us to act—books about the power of habit and inertia, probabilisms and stochastics, the theorem of Mr Thomas Bayes, cognitive psychology, behavioral economics, intrinsic reward theory, predictive analytics . . . The intellectual quest is always the same: *just why do people do the things people do*? And, for brand leaders: *can we find ingenious ways of knowing our customers better?* It's the buzz that never dies. It's the challenge re-energized as every fresh set of quarterly sales figures pops onto the Marketing Director's screen. It's that constant commercial craving to extract meaning from observation and convert it into lasting marketplace value.

Have we a line on all this to offer here? Have we a perspective sharp enough to cut down the data mound? Do we have a designer colander for sifting facts and leaving only intuitions on the table? Can we synthesize all the trends and counter-trends that our research waves confirm and purify the decisions of business strategists along the way? Can we illuminate a way through all the problems which the Jacks and Lisas of this world give, via all their overt hesitations and obscure choice-processes, to marketers and advertisers everywhere? Can we drill through the stiffer mantle and get to the core stuff?

Well, yes, we think we might be able to make a fresh, 21st century start.

Put your hand in ours.

And let us walk you down to the **Big Lie**.

Look, the 21st century consumer has one special characteristic. We call it *duxplexity*. She is capable of living in two different apartments at the same time. Our whole proposition here is that the smart brand susses this and takes advantage in the entirely legitimate pursuit of gain (improved sales, a warmer response to new product or service ideas, closer relationships all round).

In the first apartment, a noisy conversation is always taking place—a party of ideas, news and debates.

This is the place where lifestyles are reviewed and conventions confirmed, where certain views grow popular or fade from respectability, where everyone dresses as they think they should and puts up some show of social engagement. This is life as interactive hubbub, a congress of osmotic opinion-sharing sitting in permanent session, the cultural muzak we all absorb from day to day. This is: TV shows watched, celebrities admired, candidates assessed, jokes told, aspirations shared, anxieties ventilated, taboos re-affirmed, kids raised—the place where the *normal* we are all invited to respect is forged.

In the (not so much second, more the) parallel apartment, an entirely private phenomenon is at work.

Only one person lives here (well, only one *body*). And the soliloquy which she utters cannot always be heard out loud, even by her. This is the space for elemental reactions to the business of living—the purest feelings, the most uncompromising attitudes, the sharpest fears, the truest appetites. Yes, a lot of this rumbles in what used to be called the subconscious. But the tenant of this apartment, no matter what may be said aloud in the other one, is often acutely awake and alert to all that, in the end, she really wants from life and crucially *how she wants to be seen* by the outside world, ie when she throws the magic switch and re-enters the other place.

This is the **Big Lie**—the gap between social norm and private reality, between expressed opinions and inner motions, between what people say in surveys and *what their answer actually means*.

To approach modern consumers with strategic efficiency is to recognize—*to ride*—this constructive hypocrisy with which their lives are (and we use the word pointedly here) endowed. This **Big Lie** blows, like Dark Matter, through so many individual socio-economic trends and flavors the cocktail of human attitude and behavior which they describe.

Now, the really clever brand, as led by really resourceful insight professionals, intuits that the dialogue with the consumer has to take place in both apartments, in accents appropriate to each. Lisa does not want to have *no* discourse whatsoever about the social consequences of conflict diamonds or allegations about sweat shops in Bangladesh or the damage done to her neighborhood's quality of life by an over-abundance of cars. In fact, she will want to see such feelings respected at some level and in appropriate ways as she walks towards the relevant markets (or when something is bought for her).

The question though is how much are such motives *really hot* within her. She may well be the kind of person who ticks *Agree Strongly* when Future Foundation researchers ask her to respond to the statement: *I am concerned about what I can personally do to help the environment.* Or to *Global warming is really happening.* She may well be psychologically incapable of responding in any other way and it remains vitally important that such responses are measured in standard quantitative and qualitative ways. Meanwhile, Lisa would not like it if she sensed, from any quarter, that her feelings were being treated as superficial or shallow by the companies who would sell her things. But still . . . how deep is her love (for the planet)? We have to ask. We need to know.

Meanwhile, it is astonishing just how many consultancies in the field of consumer trends still advise their client brands to be—*in their immediate commercial interest*—nice, generous, open-hearted people today and all the more so tomorrow. They urge those clients to respond to *any passing expression* of intensifying human need in directly reductive ways, as if, in this line of country, two plus two really equals four.

Let's have new ultra green products. Let's provide extra in-store service assistance. Let's produce more annual reports to display our ethical practices across the world. Let's expand our conversation with customers on all social media platforms. Let's provide more salads in our restaurants. Let's talk to shoppers about how we want to build trust and transparency.

For the intelligence is that all these things are seriously wanted by this new generation of customers. So say Trends-R-Us, our consultants.

Get a life.

For us, the **Big Lie** has, in this very setting, one highly dynamic application. It reminds us that trends should not always be seen as trajectories at all but rather as moods that rise and fall. They are eminently morphable human ways of looking at life and reacting to it: sometimes thick beef stew and sometimes pink marshmallow, sometimes an exposure of the hardwiring of the consumer mind and sometimes of the capacity for the most cussèd whimsy. All trends are hallmarked by the house of Heisenberg: they are there to be measured, as best we can, in any given moment but not favored or preferred by the observer-analyst.

For when properly handled, they offer the prospect that brand leaderships can take ever more precise and ever less speculative initiatives within and on behalf of their consumer community. It is quite clear where this point, this analytical *energy* can lead. It could lead, for instance, to a corporate decision to do *less* in the field of environmental sensitivity or to withdraw certain privileges to customers (even ones they say they love)—**and not suffer any loss, however defined, whatsoever**. We, for our Future Foundation part, never forget that though we work directly for many an insight professional and marketing director they in turn go to internal meetings with Sales Directors and Finance Directors and COOs. And, given this, trends analysis has to be produced with the same detachment and discipline as quarterly sales or annual accounts. Forecasting companies should never pretend they live on sunset beach instead of the jungle, like their clients.

The cold and obvious commercial reality is that on any given day or over any given season not every product will be sold at a profit and not every inventory will be cleared from the shelves and into the hands of customers. Not every apparel product designed to appeal to, say, under-30 female professionals will recruit a good enough number of the individuals in that segment, meeting too many people who just might *not* want to follow the consumer herd but strike out on their own (in what we might call the paradox of popularity). Bad karma happens on the supply side of Main Street all the time. And, this accepted, the trends consultant should carry forward one unspoken objective all the time: to prevent the Marketing Director in the client corporation from getting fired. If he is not trying to do that then he is just a chart-hack, a brain-cluttering powerpoint concessionaire, a nice-to-have-but should-be-dropped.

Back to the **Big Lie**.

It's everywhere.

Put yourself in the position of a young sociologist recently arrived from a galaxy, far far away. He is here to complete his doctoral thesis entitled **The Uses of Social Media: an empiricist approach**. From his extensive research, he finds it passing strange that no forecaster in the 1990s actually predicted that the internet thing would become, for literally billions of earthlings, a vast human display cabinet, a continuous, often unrequested, parade of humanity's photographs, complaints, reviews, disclosures, messages, jokes . . . of the people, by the people, for the people. He has heard of the **Big Lie** theory and his observations begin to convince him that there is something it. For what greater proof of the presence of the **Big Lie** could there be than the conflicted choices the Age of Facebook drives into online lives.

*What image should I project in my **LinkedIn** page? How can I claw back pictures of myself which—though genuinely representative of a moment in my life—do not correspond to how I like to be seen by my friends today? How can I win the approval of others—both of those close to me and people I will never meet? Where is my feedback, the* *recognition of my skills as a movie critic, recipe supplier, guide to the best hotels in Barcelona, informal golf coach?*

The fact that so much of the expression of 21st century selves is *de-taggable* tells us just how malleable our personal identities are—just how we struggle to conform, struggle to individuate ourselves, struggle to "like" what we think we ought to "like". Why, on earth, would anyone want an avatar if it is not to present a different version, perhaps a truer version, of his inner life? Some business consultancies argue—and it is a widespread populist assumption too—that people just do not tell the truth in surveys and a lot of quantitative research turns easily into the strategy equivalent of junk bonds. After all, you do not need to be Nate Silver to know just how frequently election results confound even day-before predictions, especially ones based on polling data. But the story is much more subtle than this shallow presumption would imply. "Lying" is perhaps just too morally laden a term. Every time any of us answers a researcher's question or gives a co-worker an appraisal or tells a friend on **Facebook** that her prom dress is truly, truly spectacular or answers a spouse's query about the tastiness of this evening's meatloaf then the objective reality—*what do I, at heart, think and feel?*—has long since become a pretty elastic process. But *something* is revealed in every response, every remark. And often, it is our ideal self that is on guard-duty, the person we think we ought to be. To mangle a couple of old movie titles: what lies beneath is where the truth lies.

His thesis still not finished, our young sociologist heads back to Andromeda, genuinely astonished at how conflicted human beings can be, how strangely they choose, how they crave the respect of the tribe but inwardly resent the fact that they need to try. Befuddled, he looks again for the words "rational" and "self-interest" in the dictionary and cannot stop scratching his head. Just before he leaves, he watches the Demi Moore film **The Joneses**—a story about how easy it is for stealth marketers to create role models who, by their very presence in our midst, beckon us into lifestyle changes and consumption choices we did not even know we desired. From his desk, he looks up and sees his neighbors, Jack and Lisa, arguing on their front lawn. She is pointing at the new car in the driveway, clearly displeased about something. Jack has both hands above his head.

Let's re-visit some of the very stark commercial consequences of this whole thrust of argument. The value of the approach implicit in the name **"Big Lie"** is that it allows intelligence about people's lives—their expressed preferences—to be weighed and prepared for active use inside business strategy.

Let's give you an example from the United Kingdom.

It's about Christmas.

Sales Directors—in the supermarkets and department stores and bookshops and fashion outlets—live or die on the results of December trade. Oxford Street in London is a bear-pit day after day. You could fly from LAX to Heathrow in the time it would take an able-bodied person to walk, or rather push, from one end to the other any time after 1st December. It's like a month of Black Fridays. Winning the gift-hunting consumer's Christmas spend has long turned into a turf war of the utmost savagery. In January, the newspapers in Britain are always full of stories of the "high street winners", the chains that did really well, and, of course, of the brands which are, now that sales figures have been published, sadly missing in action. If a famous chain is going to go bust, there is a reasonable chance that this will happen early in any New Year. For thousands of managers in the retail trades, it really is, what a famous Scottish soccer coach calls, "squeaky bum time".

Future Foundation has for some years run an annual Christmas trends analysis program. We track what people say about their attitude to gifts, receiving and giving. We ask them what they like about the season—the parties, fun for kids, gathering the wider family around, the religious significance, etc. We also check for the incursion of other trends into the, as it were, Christmas spirit. Are people, for instance, worrying more (or less) about certain types of

Christmas activity? Is it right still to buy Christmas trees? It is right to send Christmas cards when online cards might be more eco sensitive?

And we do all this with one strategic consideration totally front of mind.

What we might loosely call social norms are more intense at Christmas time than at any other period in the year.

The British Christmas is, as a direct result, a highly conservative, conformist affair. Millions of British families do exactly the same things every time they hear them jingly bells. They eat turkey and brussels sprouts and a "pudding" so sticky and stodgy it could be used to grout bathroom tiles. They drink a truly terrible thing called mulled wine. They watch the Queen give her Christmas message on television and then settle down to repeats of comedy shows from the 1970s. The whole thing is a complete blast.

But all across Britain all year round, some of the best business brains around are plotting their brand's competitive victory for a Christmas still to come. And here are some of the questions they ask: *If we make a break for the border and offer our grocery customers something new, will they go for it? If we import fancy Christmas cakes from Canada and Brazil will they displace traditional fare (because there is an underlying, previously unanswered consumer craving for something new)?*

Putting the problem the other way round, they might also ask themselves: *If we just keep stocking all the same old stuff and avoid innovation at all costs, will we hold or perhaps increase our share (as competitor initiative-taking fails)?* This is one colossal Christmas conundrum.

So how does the theory of the **Big Lie** help here? Well, it would assist in the ordering and weighing of consumer responses to any conventionally researched interrogation of their Christmas-driven feelings. Our Future Foundation data tells us that British men are two times more likely than British women to say that they intend to buy a luxury item as a gift for their spouse/partner. (From our data archive, we have seen that this is a distribution which seems to remain stable over the years). But, at heart, how true is the story? How much do men say it—because it sounds appropriate—and how much do men *feel* it? And how might we scale the proposition against other Christmas motives: inner worries about cost outlays, buying more for the kids, the perhaps more compelling need simply to buy something new (ie not bought in previous years) or, alternatively, conventional (jewelry, **Chanel No 5** . . .)?

Indeed the challenge for the trends analyst becomes positively atomic. What *is* Christmas? In the emotional eco-system of the consumer, what purpose does it serve? Why, for instance, is there an explosion of nostalgia and sentimentality in every December? When we ask British people what they like most about the season they say that *it's a time when the whole family gets together,* a feature which far outstrips, say, *going to Christmas parties.* It is right to assume that there has to be a measure of contrived mendacity at work here or merely a sense of being pre-programmed into taking certain opinions, *officially* feeling a lot of something (but *unofficially* feeling perhaps a lot less in the privacy of one's mind), letting social norms do our thinking for us. And sorting all this so that communications are perfected and products improved or changed is absolutely the strategic commercial task. Consumers, at some station inside themselves, have to be induced to conclude that, by the fullest content of identity and offer, this company or this brand really understands them as they search for their big tickets and their stocking fillers.

In the sense we use here, Christmas is full of lies.

This leads to a final thematic.

The reality of globalization has beckoned forth a range of international trends monitoring services. Big brands, as they stretch around the planet, crave economies of scale. They need to find ideas that can work (if not everywhere then) in as many places as possible without alteration. We speak here of advertising concepts, corporate identity programs, PR executions, product and service innovations . . . And so, those brands naturally turn to the forecasting community in search of compelling stories about how our 8 billion neighbors are living their lives now and how those lives might be changing.

Converging? Diverging? Suitable for regional but not global interpretation? Americanizing? Europeanizing? Gender-equalizing? Liberalizing? Wanting the same fun? Demanding the same quality-of-life agenda? Worrying about the same things? Becoming more capricious, less *rational*? It's not just Jack and Lisa we must get to know. But also Lukas and Sofie. And Luiza and João Pedro. And Yousouf and Fatima. And Xiu Li and Jianguo. And Thierry and Nicolas. How to measure the structural forces in so many lives, all the things that individuals cannot change on their own account—the politics, the geography, the demographics, the weather in the streets? How to measure the discretionary opportunities they genuinely enjoy, opportunities to create the lifestyles they truly want?

*And how to know just how much of the **Big Lie** is present and active in their lives?*

The answer to such questions can never be a list. Never an indigestible dagwood of bar charts. Never just another bulging, barely downloadable update for the poor encumbered client to try to convert into meaning. The number of data points in any global quantitative survey becomes a gloriously exponential distribution. To assess the penetration of a particular trend from country to country becomes, mentally, something of an extreme sport. Sometimes, it feels like a native Quechua speaker being invited to translate Sanskrit poetry into Finnish. But the translation has to be done.

Let's take an example. From our researches, we know that there seem to be quite seriously different approaches to, for instance, the definition of luxury in Japan as against India and China. Elsewhere, around 6% of young people in Japan tell us they are angry about any excessive, environmentally insensitive packaging of goods. The figure is over 30-40% among the middle-classes of India and China. Generally, eco-worries of a kind which place a real pressure on companies to go ever greener seem to be just not as intense in Japan as they are in other parts of the world. On another theme, in the division of household responsibilities (cleaning, cooking, garbage management . . .), Japanese men seem to be living in a society as different to Sweden as Mercury is to Pluto.

(We discuss the relevance and the application of Globally Adjusted Data in the final section of this book. Our own approach to GAD permits a more nuanced perspective on what are apparently extreme differences in consumer opinions from country-to-country. More on this later.)

Now, we talk here so far *only about what people say in response to questions from our researchers*. Of course, we have to, exploiting other sources, find out all we can about the other motive forces driving each society forward, know the big facts-and-figures, read books and blogs, listen to our trendspotters (and, incidentally, people in business too). All our trends must be ignited by a continuous fuel-injection of fresh and workable hypotheses about what they, in interaction with themselves and across the continents, actually mean. How efficiently do they really capture all the relevant elements of consumer attitude and behavior in one useful bundle of thought?

Trends analysis thus becomes one long propositional calculus. It just has to get *smarter* all the time, if it is to meet the demands of brands, young and established, which want to straddle the planet and see profits cubed. For some time now, our Future Foundation teams have been growing new and ever more sophisticated applications of conjoint and related techniques in order to meet just such an agenda. This is done with, critically, the precept of the **Big Lie** in mind. We set out to fashion a working model of how consumer-citizens in an integrating international economy react to questions about their lives, of where and why they would evade disclosure, of just how *programatically* they react to the wisdom of the social crowds around them and of how they like to be addressed and reassured and persuaded.

Global trends analysis is facing intense pressure to prove its power to forecast. It is, long since, not good enough to be *interesting* any more. If such analysis is not helping to swell a bottom line somewhere down the track then it is simply not worth the investment. It is time for those involved in such analysis to build their own equivalent to Silicon Valley and to invent the mental software which lets all those who need to plan on a global scale at least glimpse the future *with some chance of influencing it in their favor.*

We believe that the theory of the **Big Lie** brings a power-tool to the table.

But for now we have to get back to Jack and Lisa. To find that present, Jack is heading to a specialist bookstore in Inner Richmond.

And it is, as it were, his own Inner Richmond which interests us, Future Foundation, very much indeed.

Imagine that.

We call our book the **Big Lie**. This is a deliberately controversial title and we address the theme especially to the business community and to the imperative to create communication campaigns and supply products which tap into consumers' realities as well as their projected personas. Consumers need to feel good on two levels—something we call the duality of marketing. The smart brand has to respect social norms but address the real feelings and needs which lie underneath. Our proposition is that consumers, consciously or unconsciously, are happy to go along with this.

In addition:

- We want to pull the lives of global consumers into the sharpest possible focus.
- We believe that the **Big Lie** represents an entirely justifiable comment on those lives.
- We see success swelling for consumer-facing brands to the extent that they are able to speak to the social being and the private being, the projected self and the hidden *me* without confusion or contradiction—in sensitivity-with-a-purpose.
- We know that the **Big Lie** is a potent way of organizing / prioritizing social trends inside commercial strategy.

The **Big Lie** concept—and the tracking of social norms that it demands—drives ever more sophisticated questioning of consumers and supports, from trend to trend, a social-norms indexing of individual countries; in this way, geography dies and ever more colorful, ever more informative segmentations of populations can be mapped.

CHAPTER ONE

EVER SMARTER CONSUMERS, ENDLESSLY IRRATIONAL CHOICES

Questions for Analysis

- Much is written about the tendency for consumers to behave in ways which do not obviously appear to be in their best interests. What should we make of this phenomenon and can the **Big Lie** thesis explain it—and indeed put it to good use inside commercial strategy?
- How easy is it for consumers to be honest with those who would sell them things and why should they bother to explore and accurately define their own feelings?

- Can you, the nicest and most well-meaning brand in the universe, ever be your customers' friend? Does it matter that they may never be prepared to fully trust you? Will you ever be able to sit and drink coffee together, laugh out loud at the same things?
- Some analysts speak of the "death of narrativity", a consequence of living in the cold Age of Digital. Does this actually widen the opportunity for brands to have perfectly *irrational* but perfectly fruitful conversations with consumers? Do **Big Lie** circumstances mean better prospects for brands which want to tell stories and worry less about functional claims of value-for-money?
- Brand managers everywhere get frustrated at the reality of the under-engaged (and therefore perhaps indeed irrational) consumer. How can trends analysis, influenced by the **Big Lie** proposition and a sharpened awareness of prevailing social norms, deepen insight and re-tool commercial strategy in such circumstances?

Taking one for the team

Modern consumerism is, as we insight professionals might simplify it in our minds, a game played between two teams. The personnel on each side changes every second. Some leave the field of play for a while to come back mostly for the big ticket moments. Some track what is happening during the match with military, minute-to-minute scrutiny and make their move at the very last opportunity. Sometimes, players get distracted, make mistakes, drop the ball. Often, bitter complaints about refereeing decisions can be heard. But generally everyone knows both the rules and the intrinsic nature of the game. Sometimes you win, sometimes you lose and sometimes it is just a drawn-out draw. And there is one salient feature, easily noted to be significant by a visiting professor of Earthling Studies:

team objectives and strategies are not to be broadcast. The game is not played for fun or to bring entertainment to the crowd; the goal to is use what resources are available, sometimes sneakily if necessary, to take the day. Or, to break the metaphor, to have the market *clear* in your favor.

All consumer markets run on the basis of limited disclosure and contrived display. This is very much the way we all live, under the umbrella of the **Big Lie**.

How many in our midst have ever walked into a department store to say to the nice sales assistant: *I need to buy a present for my wife but such has been my outlay this month—what with the new car and all—that I am seriously short of cash. So, I need an expensive-looking bracelet or necklace.*

Way too much information there, however true it is.

Meanwhile, no department store manager ever uses the public address system to announce: *Visit our cosmetics counters today. You will find them specially lit to exaggerate our customers' personal attractiveness, such as it is. The nice fragrance you smell has been specially disseminated because it has been proven, in clinical trials with guinea pig shoppers, to beckon both male and female customers from all over the store. Some products are displayed inside a locked glass cabinet—this is to make you feel that they are extra-special and worthy of the extra-special price tag.*

Way too much information there, however true it is.

In spite of what life-coaches might say on daytime television, every relationship tolerates only so much honesty. And it is on this strange form of energy that our **Big Lie** runs. The dialogue between buyer and supplier so often becomes a curtain holed by half-truths and second-guessings. The buyer assumes that the supplier exists to maximize profits; the supplier assumes that the buyer wants all goods at squeezed margins. Look at the crowds that rush like long-starved zombies into big fashion outlets when the immediately overwhelmed security man opens the doors on the first day of sales. Look at the hotels which adjust their prices whenever travel disruption detains thousands more business-people in a city than would normally be the case. What does such behavior suggest to us? That market players—perhaps all of them—will exploit situations if they can? Bet your bottom dollar.

> "I believe it is a game of Beat-the-Retailer. It's always good to find a bargain. It gives you a sense of victory".
>
> **Female, 30, finance director, Dallas, TX, USA**

A man finds himself in an ethnic restaurant in San Francisco. He notices there is a bottle of wine, the name scrawnily handwritten on tonight's menu, priced at $12. It is a **Gevrey-Chambertin**, Premier Cru, 2006. This just has to be a pricing mistake—either that or the wine has rotted and is being dumped this very evening on unsuspecting diners. What is Jack to do? What is, to begin to open our theme here, the *rational* thing for him *qua* consumer to do? All might seem fair in love and wonton. He orders the whole bottle (though he really wants only a glass), tastes it and knows instantly that the pinot is absolutely delicious and ludicrously under-priced. When the nice manager later asks him if everything is good with his meal, Jack nods vigorously and says nothing. He scored a big point tonight. Got one over on the other team. Makes up for being ripped-off so often. Blaaah!

Now, of course, some of us would have argued all night with the restaurant manager that he must immediately charge at least $100 for the top class Burgundy red. The manager, confused and somehow insulted, might well have eventually asked us to leave.

Our point is that brands and consumers alike *generally* communicate in a culture and conspiracy of self-interest, a kind of aisle-dance of the seven veils, always under-revealing some motives and some tastes. There is something incongruous if not downright inelegant about a consumer wanting to play, even from the best of motives, for the other team. The staff at your local supermarket do not volunteer information about the best place to get good deals on personal electronics elsewhere in the precinct, do they? And if, while TV-dinner browsing, you were approached by one of them to be whispered that lasagne A is *s**t* but lasagne B is really tasty and offering excellent value-for-money then you might well conclude that this was nothing more a shabby attempt to manipulate, a cheap marketing trick. The supplier is just not meant to be your friend. And it is a bit of a **Big Lie** on its own that he ever can be. Though marketing guide-books rarely spell it out, there is, from the souk to the mall, something quintessentially and permanently *adversarial* in the play of sell-and-buy.

All of this is precisely what makes quantitative research activity still so valuable and so fascinating. And valuable and fascinating too what brands choose to say about themselves—their goals, their missions, their core competences—in corporate propaganda. For smart brands know that, just like them vaudeville prestidigitators of old, consumers are capable of quite elaborate schemes of misdirection within what they say about themselves and their appetites. Much marketing success can turn on the pro-active appreciation of this very truth. For this truth, incidentally, can pave the way to some *apparently* irrational or at least unstable behavior on the part of even astute and assured consumers.

Any reason to assume that consumers reason any more / any less than economists do?

It is indeed the case that workaday economists and other analyst tribes, as many commentators of the modern era have observed, were once wont to over-define the rationality of the everyday consumer—in as much as they made the word mean: *doing all that is necessary as a market agent to maximize, from decision to decision, the returns to me*. This was and indeed remains the crux of **Rational Choice Theory**, an approach which might once have explained how markets work just as old man Ptolemy might once have explained how heavenly bodies really move. The idea that market players (aka consumers) are always ready-and-equipped to maximize the utility of any situation in their favor has long since been dented by developments in psychology, sociology and by the general thrust of what is these days called Behavioral Economics. But maximizing can take many chameleon forms, as we shall presently discuss.

This takes us along a short tangent. Have we noticed just how hard it is for even very smart people pithily to describe what is truly happening at the moment when an object becomes a possession, when a sale is made? Milton Friedman apparently once said: *"The most important single central fact about a free market is that no exchange takes place unless both parties benefit"*. One of the brains behind Guerrilla Marketing apparently once said: *"In order to sell a product or a service, a company must establish a relationship with the consumer. It must build trust and rapport. It must understand the customer's needs, and it must provide a product that delivers the promised benefits"*. Marketing gurudom is top-to-bottom upholstered by catchpenny quotes like this, quotes which doubtless find their way into a thousand undergraduate dissertations every day.

But, if we poke through the verbal skin here, what is the nature of "benefit" and how stable is that nature? How would Milton's dictum adequately cope with a phenomenon like *Freemium*? It would presumably have been tricky for him to deal with **Wikipedia**, the buckshee knowledge-bomb that killed **Encarta**. Or, for that matter, **Facebook**. From his worldview too, it was always going to be hard to predict a phenomenon like **TripAdvisor**. Lots of exchange with no money changing hands.

Meanwhile, if one *and only one* airline flies direct from my home city to Geneva and I really want to ski down Mont Blanc this Winter, how much "trust and rapport" needs to exist before I buy a ticket? *Hardly any at all*: is the practical answer. Could it ever come to pass that the "promised benefits"—the benefits illuminated in advertising campaigns and promotional language—are not actually the benefits the consumer privately craves (as the brand-owner often understands perfectly well)? We mean no disrespect to Messrs Friedman and Co—and others who over the years have supplied the Bumper Book of Quickfire Marketing Quotations—but do statements like the above, even for the time they were written, really cut it? Or, to mangle something King Claudius says, are they much too lightly timbered for the loud winds that blow through the actual moment of 21st century consumer choice?

In their otherwise diverting book, **Drinking From The Fire Hose** (subtitled: *Making smarter decisions without drowning in information*), Christopher J Frank and Paul Magnone talk at one point on the theme of *building brand health*. The text at one point runs:

".. . *it's important to remember that every customer has a specific set of needs the product must satisfy. The ability of the brand and the product to meet these needs is the key to market success and consumer loyalty. If your company's image is closely associated with the drivers of choice, there is a higher probability that your product will be included in that buyer's consideration set—or the set of products and services the customer will consider buying".*

That the book containing this quote was published as late as 2011 is striking. To us writing here as the proponents of the **Big Lie**, statements like this perpetuate the illusion that there is something which can be very easily settled and simplified inside the play of consumer values, consumer needs. They seem designed to shoo away human complexity and the multiple dualisms which we present across our whole **Big Lie** proposition.

Let's think about it. Under what conceivable conditions is a customer's "set of needs" specific to the point of and in the sense of being permanently stable and static? Are those needs revealed as truths which stand proud at every time of day and in all foreseeable circumstances? Are those needs never confounded by sheer cussedness, casual forgetfulness or pure laziness?

On a simple reading, the quote we relay above seems like ordinary wisdom but the very notion of the "drivers of choice" itself just cannot be a lapidary, hard-set state of affairs. The "set of needs", meanwhile, can be so many vibrating strings, signals from parallel universes of motive and appetite, not representing any kind of unitary commercial gravity at all. And sometimes, of course, consumers do actually buy what they buy and say what they say under the influence of their peers and networks and other social forces. Sometimes they need to conform to certain attitudes just as much as they need to procure certain possessions. In such conditions, *rationality* is hard both to define and identify. There is *a kind of* reasoning lying behind my choice of car when I am more motivated by what my friends will think of my choice than I am by the objective qualities of the marque in question. It is at some level logical *enough* regularly to visit a hamburger restaurant and one day tell a telephone pollster that you think that the company concerned is a rip-off merchant with a very un-praiseworthy record on environmental issues—while (with good reasons of personal convenience in mind) not changing or planning for one minute to change your regular choice of lunch venue.

> "I have never paid much attention to brands. I go more for the product I am looking for then go by price or if I think a customer service person seems genuine I will listen to them. Nine times out of ten I know what I want and will look up reviews on them and go from there. I have never been really disappointed with a product I have bought".
>
> **Female, 35-44, married, 2 children, Australia**

Big Business must be Bad Business

Around this point, there is a constant provocation of examples. In Future Foundation surveys, just short of 70% of Americans agree with the statement: *I wish big companies were more prepared to apologize in public when things go wrong.* Is this figure a cumulative representation of the direct personal opinions of millions of individual citizens or essentially a *social* view, the kind of opinion that most folks would share and voice in conversation? (Only 2% of the Americans we survey disagree strongly with the statement). Well, it is emphatically a heavily socialized assumption not to trust anyone who is trying to sell you something and to be generally suspicious of big business.

Consider the long list of movies which over the years have had, as the mainspring of their plot, the easily triggered duplicitousness or outright beastliness of big business. *The China Syndrome? Silkwood? Wall Street? Erin Brockovich? A Civil Action? The Smartest Guys in the Room? The Constant Gardner? Avatar? Michael Clayton? Duplicity? Up in the Air? Love and Other Drugs? Margin Call? The Promised Land? The Truth?*

The impact of this deeply ingrained cultural motif is on its own powerful enough to make it perhaps seem uncomfortable for people to say out loud in conversation that big companies in America—the most pro-business society on earth—have no real need to apologize for anything and should just get on with doing business as they see fit. But our private views and impulses—the ones that lead to actual choices and behaviors—are so frequently a different cup of meat, one not always teased into full view by market research questioning. From day to day, one may like to hear big business act humble and one may be outraged by any overt expression of corporate arrogance. But away from the social conversation referenced here, is one often driven to reject or switch or boycott individual brands if their actions fall below expected standards? *Rarely*: seems to be the answer. From a distance, this actually might seem psychologically dissonant, even irrational. But it is very much the way we live—inside a volatile mix of social interaction and private impulse, not always aware ourselves of the imbrication between the two.

At this point, it is important to stress that we are not arguing that the **Big Lie** is a new continent that we have just discovered. Many successful consumer companies have long since rumbled the fundamental precepts of our theme without necessarily defining it as we do here or proving its existence and value through the examples we offer or generally using the language we use. Perhaps some actually just apply **Big Lie** ideas without realizing it. But we certainly do offer the **Big Lie** as, we hope, a refreshing antidote to anodyne marketing advice.

Kill the cliché before it kills you

If you were to reflect on the quotation above (from Frank & Magnone) and so many others like it freely available on a bookstand near you, you might well ask yourself how well its content will capture, say, the business of setting out to buy a birthday present for someone whom a young woman has just recently started dating. Or how a new kitchen is to be presented and offered to a newly married couple who have no idea about what to buy, how much to pay, how to arrange the fitting (but will not say any of these things out loud—even to each other). Buying an item, almost any item, is what learned academics often call a *social construct*. Any suggestion that an individual shopper and a particular brand directly talk to each other in totally dis-intermediated accents right up to the moment of purchase (or not) as if inside a soundproof room must be wrong. There is always a crowd at the checkout.

Of course, many purchase moments are perfectly, repetitiously banal. A man has a headache; lots of noisy exchanges on the home front have recently taken a toll. He drives straight down to **Rite Aid** (visited many times before with many successful outcomes—besides, likes the pharmacist, name of Selena) to buy some **Advil** (always worked effectively in the past). The "set of needs" (pain, discomfort) and the "drivers of choice" (familiarity, convenience) seem in pleasingly logical alignment. Prevailing social norms infiltrate into the moment but lightly, if at all—a common function, one might conclude, in distress purchases of all sorts. But in so much of 21st century consumption and life, the active choices that reveal one's attitudes—or could potentially reveal one's prejudices, one's hesitations, one's inadequacies, one's capacity to act in sub-rational ways—are arguably more numerous and more public than they have ever been.

A young woman enters a department store with the intention of buying a suit for a vitally important job interview which is imminent. Lisa has, so it seems, certain rough choice criteria in her mind: something conservative, expensive-looking, emitting a signal of cool proficiency within the wearer. As she tries various possibilities in the changing room, she starts zipping photos of herself to her **Facebook** page to generate responses, suggestions, critiques from pre-warned friends. As these start to arrive, the result is a splash after splash of conflicting advice from across her social network; many are urging her to buy the super-expensive **Dolce & Gabbana** but her instinct (not conveyed to her audience) is to prefer the store's own-label alternative which is $200 cheaper. The shop assistant who is a real pain in the *a*s* keeps pushing the same single-breasted, front-closure number with dual back vents—the own-label option. So irritating is she (with her barely disguised promotional and probably commission-inspired agenda) that Lisa determines not to purchase it even though it is the one she prefers. Suddenly a text arrives from a friend with certain oft-ventilated political attitudes who urges no commerce with any brand which employs sweat-shop labor in Asia; Lisa responds by agreeing that this has to be an important consideration. Next there is a phone call from another gal-pal offering to lend Lisa an old thing she has in her closet from the **Tom Ford** label which may fit the interview moment and save her some serious outlay. Lisa gets tired, switches off her cell, grabs the **D&G** and pays for it quickly.

So, how would we define or describe the *utility function* which inhabited Lisa's ultimate choice? How many different strands of potential rationality were present as she processed her options? Even the term *bounded rationality* (favored by some economists) barely covers what took place. And if she were asked by an opinion researcher why she picked the **D&G** suit, would she mention—*would she be able to recall/ would she want to recall*—everything that transpired?

How many assets can be kept in trust?

It is extraordinary, while we linger here, how many analysts still act as if and argue that markets cannot function without the presence of widespread trust. In fact, there is something of an interesting dialectic here. Marketing consultants, the supporters who fill the stadium, as it were, of Team Brand, vaunt *trust* as both a virtue and an asset and tell companies to seek it and to grow it. Elsewhere, for the broad community of consumers, it is regarded as wise and self-preservational *not* to implicitly trust the people on the other side of the counter. Lots of warnings are shared every day as consumers who have suffered bad experiences tell folks they do not personally know: *Do not buy a policy from this insurer—they will not pay out / Do not stay at that hotel—the brochure does not tell you that it is a two mile walk through steaming sewage to reach the beach / Do not order that movie—the promise in the trailer of "many scenes of sizzling eroticism" is a complete fabrication.*

In our Future Foundation global research program, we ask questions like: *How much do you trust retailers in general to do business fairly?* Perhaps our readers will not be surprised to learn that the proportion answering *very much* in any given corner of the world is miniscule. Around 5% in the US and UK. Less than 20% of Americans tell us that they *trust airlines to do business fairly* either *very much* or *quite a lot.* Less than 40% of Americans say that they *trust their supermarkets to charge fair prices.* None of this in any way interdicts the year on year—downturns apart—swelling in the purchase of clothes and air travel and fine foods. It is the primary social norm, the first commandment, of consumerism that suppliers of all kinds are to be universally mistrusted—even as millions of us continue to shop in the same old, same old places every month in life. Inertia is so frequently a greater market dynamic—hardly the word perhaps—than pro-active trust. Many a, say, financial services company knows this all too keenly. But is this ever said out loud and in public? No.

"As far as trusting advice given by banks, that would be a NO! I am just a realist. A realist is a cynic with a lot of experience. lol I am not very trusting of any bank".

Male, 62, grandfather, Charlotte, NC, USA

Often, consultants from the PR universe will make much of the need for companies to accumulate trust assets. But it is quite easy to imagine circumstances under which such an effort will simply be a waste of corporate energy, in as much as profits will not really be left any more protected as a result. Imagine a country in which only five banks are allowed (or have the commercial capacity) to offer checking account products. Imagine that all the employees in that country have their salaries paid directly, whether they like it or not, into their bank accounts each month. Imagine further that when asked whether they actually trusted the bank community in their country, 75% of consumer-citizens emphatically disagreed. In such conditions—not so far from reality in much of the Western world—the fact that the trust assets are so weak will make precious little difference to market behaviors from week to week.

Consider. I have a favorite candy bar. Do I suspect that the manufacturer will sneakily reduce the size of the bar every now and then to reduce costs? Yes, I do. Will I stop buying the candy bar? No, I will not. A lot of consumption is just like stalemate. Few may be perfectly happy with the outcome; nobody wants to stop the game.

"Over the past year, I have noticed many items, such as ice cream and tissues, have downsized their serving size. However the cost has stayed the same. I have emailed these companies letting them know my displeasure".

Female, 43, postgraduate, Northeast suburbs, USA

For the consumer, perfect is often not worth the price

Over the years, the intellectual slow-train of super-rationality (ie everything must have an obvious purpose of immediate transactional coherence) has led—not so much these days perhaps—to some very static, linear and ultra-orthodox advice to companies as they try to build credibility and affection for their brands. The *maximizing-market-agent* definition is, of course, as weak as it looks. For no consumer alive could possibly process every single moment of decision into a perfect outcome. And the word "perfect" is hardly a simple, stable condition anyway. This reality actually leads in itself to some perfectly logical but practically imperfect behavior on the part of consumers everywhere.

For instance, anyone searching for ice cream for two grumpy toddlers at a seaside resort on a stinking hot day will probably *not* spend too much time comparing prices at the competing stalls or checking out every conceivable combination of flavors and sundaes. As the sweat mats the hair to your head, your two much-loved daughters will be given, once the end of the line is finally reached, precisely five seconds to confirm their choice. Later that day, suddenly on the verge of running out of gas on the interstate, you will probably *not* take a moment to reflect on the environmental policies of the competing oil companies or even their record, as much as you can recollect it, in keeping prices low for hard-pressed Middle-American families like yourself. The only smart thing to do is to fill the tank full of whatever brand of gas you can find as soon as possible. To misquote the man from **Zen and the Art of Motorcycle Maintenance,** rationality is not a skill or a condition or an imperative. It is an *event*. It is *circumstantial*. It *all depends*.

From our global Future Foundation data, we know that around three-quarters of Americans and similar proportions of, say, French and German consumers will agree that they *shop around extensively to get the best deals*. We are hardly surprised that this is such a common motivation; it sounds like common sense and it would be regarded as eccentric by those in your social circle for you not to subscribe to it. Even billionaires will never tell a researcher—if one ever reaches them—that they simply ignore the cost of heating their homes or flying their planes. We are all culturally locked into formally expressed price sensitivity, whatever our actual behavior from market to market.

> "It is absolutely essential that I try to save money while shopping. Salaries are not rising, but food costs definitely are. I usually go on-line or look in the circular to see what is on sale at my regular food store, and make my list accordingly. Then I also go through my coupons and see which ones I can use. If I need something specific, and it is not on sale at my regular store but another one, I will go to the other store to buy it".
>
> **Female, 43, Northeast, USA**

So, how then—residual oligopolistic situations apart—does any thick price premium ever manage to survive? How come this apparent intensity of focus on price seems often to slacken and dissipate? Why do discount houses not rule the earth? Why is it so hard for brands to die? Is it possible for some offers to sustain an apparently open dialogue about money—acknowledging that prices must be kept low—while inter-communicating with consumers about other issues in a more oblique, possibly subterranean way. Of course. This is precisely how the world works.

Consider in this dimension the 21st century phenomenon of **Native Marketing**. Really adventurous brands seem to have heard the populist clamor that the Digital Age has no soul; that human connections have been generally enfeebled under the self-imposed, obsessive slavery that is life with the solitary screen; that we have lost from our days what some call *narrativity*—the sense that life is not just about immediate functionality but a business which needs stories and myths as much as ever.

Native Marketing is an approach which pitches the brand as often something seriously *de-producted*, ie something now taking the primary role of stockbroker of information, advice, discussion, topic-management. The conversation is not or rarely turning on the price and quality and value-for-money of the service originally offered but rather on, well, life itself and the issues of the day.

Life runs more on narrative than on function

The **Coca Cola** pages on **Facebook**—which forum environmental issues, Mark Ronson gigs, sports days, photo collections . . .—are a brilliant example of a brand-consumer dialogue just about as remote from a conventional shopping experience as flying business class is to commuting on the subway. The pages from the Spanish retailer **El Corte Inglés** are little more than a magazine for discussing and sharing ideas about fashions, foods and lifestyles. The website of a brand like **Smirnoff** is a riff on all the possibilities of nightlife everywhere—all delivered with limited and indeed occasional references to vodka. The sell is so soft you could put your kids down to sleep on it.

> "I like shopping at El Corte Inglés, a Spanish department store, I like El Corte Inglés that has a lot of leading brands, many vendors who will advise and solve your problems and also can order anything that is not sold in the shop without additional cost, it is also a company with many years of experience and well established in the Spanish society, to sum up, offer good services and are close to the customer (sic)".
>
> **Male, 16-24, father, smartphone owner, Spain**

With so many links, clips, podcasts, photo- and opinion-sharing over so many interconnected platforms, such brands fit flowingly round the contours of consumers' lives, constantly and often almost hypnotically re-inventing new forms of relevance for themselves. Of course, many brands still cling like barnacles to a messaging language, even in cyber space, that is really so much rehashed, in-store promotional pitching—the *see here for high quality products at affordable prices* variety. And there are truly many market situations still when one's employee's job is to brutally concentrate on persuading truculent shoppers and, in entirely 20th century *hurry-while-stocks-last ways*, get the shampoo and the children's shoes and the sunglasses off the shelves and into the shopping bags.

But, alongside and above this, the Digital Revolution gives brands so many more and richer opportunities to get consumers talking with them about life and color and entertainment and things that matter both a little and sometimes a lot. It's capitalism, Jim, but not entirely as Adam Smith and his hidden hand once knew it—or for that matter, the marketing gurus of the last century. The absolute concentration on the optimized deal, the shaking of hands, the cash nexus . . . is not what it was, in spite of what consumer-citizens tell opinion researchers. In this very direct sense, consumers get *more* irrational rather than less.

Listen.

When the sales and marketing team behind the clothing lines launched by, say, Sofia Vergara or Jennifer Lopez shift their product and sit down to assess quarterly revenues, what is that they, on reflection, think they are selling? Mere dresses and leggings and accessories? Or all these things reinforced by something intangible and ethereal—an implied connection to beauty, celebrity and fun?

If a soccer fan is able to buy a season ticket to watch the home matches of the world's biggest club, **Manchester United**, is the end-product just a fortnightly, ninety-minute football game? Or an invigorated sense of tribal belonging? The chance to sing songs and, embracing fellow fans whose name you do not even know, shed tears of legitimized manliness on the day when one final score brings the trophy home? (The singer Marie Osmond, no less, is a fan of **Kilmarnock Football Club** in Scotland. The club's supporters often deliver a lusty *a cappella* version of her hit *Paper Roses* during matches. The relevance of this ritual to the football itself is, of course, nil).

Is a thing like **Johnnie Walker Platinum Label** really a blended scotch whisky at all any more? Or rather a special kind of passport for those who own it, show it and serve it in their homes? A benediction of exclusivity and discernment? Most emphatically.

At the brand brainstorming with the ad agency, you do not need to have Don Draper in the house to drive the big question: *With this skin cream range/greetings cards series/hotel chain/lingerie store . . . what is it, in this decade and in this consumer culture, that we are actually selling these days?* For all the purposeful, review-assisted, price-comparing shopping taking place in the 21st century, the answer to any such question is rarely: a piece of fruit, a shirt, an object.

Markets run on an enormous amount of unspoken and often un-named consumer motive.

I might well say I much admire **American Apparel** because its website allows me to check out the company's labor practices on a live feed—but only if the question is so framed to prompt me to think about that very subject. Unprompted, the only admiring remark I might make about the brand is that its summer-wear does indeed make me look a bit thinner. But I may not admit even that. If ever asked, I might well tell anyone (an acquaintance, a researcher, someone met on vacation . . .) that I follow **Game of Thrones** because of the gripping disquisition on the Machiavellian realities of political power that is detectable under the dialogue. The fact that many of the actors are so breath-curtailingly beautiful that I could *so* never ever miss an episode is not a fact to be ventilated; it might make me seem trite. More, I might well go fine-dining in new French restaurants in Russian Hill in order, primarily, to be able to post a review of the *foie gras mousse* the following day and thus achieve the status of food critic. Called at home by a market research agency, I might well agree that the most attractive feature of **McDonald's** is indeed the general cleanliness of the store when the fact that my nearest branch is only 100 meters from my apartment is actually the handy heart of the matter. The onion of motive has to be peeled, 360 degrees at a time. This is the **Big Lie** mindset and imperative.

Reasons to be prosperous

Often enough, consumers are positively stimulated to be irrational—irrational in the sense of not focusing exclusively or necessarily on their long-term interests as market agents. It may sound cold when said aloud but those in the commercial insight trades *who do well* invariably proceed on the basis of a finely-tuned detachment in the face of what consumers say to researchers—especially when the questions touch, let's call it, their own consumer *virility*, their own ability to insist on a good deal, to see through the marketer's wiles, to assess value on the basis of their own experience and general lifestyle savviness. A famous French business guru once defined marketing as—we translate freely here—*the continuous re-seduction of the potentially promiscuous*. And those shoppers who are in the market for that good deal today may well over-estimate their capacity to resist ever more sophisticated versions of the seducer's craft.

Once again, it's not that opinion research is terminally shallow in the answers it provides; it's not that the quant excel spreadsheet should be left on the margins of strategic insight discussion. Just the opposite. All responses to questions are bountiful in what they reveal about a) what consumers think they ought to say b) how they will reply under certain circumstances and in certain moments c) whether specific social norms seem to be gaining or losing potency in the life of the nation. To some extent, respondents will always see the market research interview as some kind of exam in which they must, if necessary, grope for the *right* answers—since the answers will all add up to a commentary on their smartness, their talent, their whole status in the world. How many of us will tell a stranger that we hardly ever clean our kitchen sink?

Over the years, Future Foundation has worked alongside hundreds and hundreds of senior professionals from one corner or another of the insight and persuasion businesses. It is striking how often such professionals have a passion for what they are selling—the kitchen cleaner, the mobile handset, the exotic holiday, the living room fabrics, the value-for-money groceries, the TV channel, the sports kit . . . They genuinely want the consumer to buy their stuff because they think their stuff is good. (We occasionally meet hard-boiled cynics who would treat their customers as easily drugged laboratory animals. These people can hardly ever be assisted in their commercial goals by trends analysis. And they often—no cheap shot here—do not do well). But our passionate insight colleagues seem to know that they are engaged in a kind of benevolent conspiracy against the consumers they would like to hold or recruit. Consider, with this very thought, the degree to which the techniques of espionage and surveillance have penetrated the marketing approach, the salesperson's profession.

As a famous Belgian detective might well say, this is a subject so delicate. Over the years, brand owners and shop owners—always searching for that silver bullet—have turned to the varied promises of ethnographic research, filmed shopper behavior, body-language reading, synaesthesic and sensorial marketing, decoy effect pricing, behavioral economics, predictive analytics . . . all in the name of so framing the moment of choice that the dice are weighed in their favor.

The case of the under-engaged customer

One rarely hears the question asked: *what do consumers themselves think of all this?* All this *contrivance*. All the money spent on marketing buzz and nudge and all that clever jazz. Well, we should readily assume that consumers know that it is all out there. They know that the pastel-colored sweaters in fashion displays are deliberately lit in a certain alluring way; they know that previous movie purchases are scanned in order to perfect online promotional targeting for new releases; they know that they are being filmed (and not for security reasons) as they mentally flick through all the types of orange juice on display in store and as they discuss and argue final choices with their kids. In a funny way, it is right to conclude that consumers think this is simply what marketers do. Perhaps it would be rational if they paid more attention to the devices used while taking time to read the marketing press and the journals of market research societies to learn of the latest ones in play. But this would require too much energy and would, somehow, break the rules of the game. Not for the first time in our **Big Lie** story, much of what actually occurs in the relationship between customer and supplier is left unsaid or at least under-mentioned.

It is not *that* often that a particular purchase engages every muscle in the consumer's heart and head.

Somewhere out there, a marketing manager is pretty well obsessed by the performance of the brand of personal deodorant which he runs, obsessed by the success of the advertising investment, impact of price changes and promotions, tracking of PR campaigning, protection of a positioning specially crafted against competitors . . . He even brings his charts home to show his long-suffering wife.

Now, he knows that his target consumer—from, say, the constituency of men under-30—usually spends 6-8 seconds in-aisle selecting which brand of deodorant he is going to buy. He knows that for as long as the price over the counter remains competitive, 75% of those who bought the brand last month will buy it this month too. This is commercially satisfactory but our brand manager wishes his customer could be a bit more enthusiastic, just a bit more *engaged*. However, the market is not a high motivator for the average American twenty-something. Clint does not, it is true, want to smell like stale minestrone when out on a date. But this is still a relatively low-interest purchase story for him. In fact, it would be positively *anti*-irrational for him to know the names and the prices and the ingredients of all the anti-perspirant deodorants on the market. At dinner, what man is going to start talking to his date about the competing virtues of **Old**

Spice and **Speed Stick** and **Crystal Body Travel Stick**? If he does, he is just never going to get the chance to steer the conversation to *Fifty Shades* as he would like to do—because the date will be terminated with extreme prejudice. Simon & Garfunkel never wrote songs about the thrill of shopping for good-quality hardwood flooring. Adele's song is not: *Someone Like You, My Realtor.*

> "I am in no way loyal to any brands. It has nothing to do with bargains, or popular name brands. If I like something, I'm sure something out there will perform just as good. I'm racking my brain to find something that I will continue to buy because of a brand name, or because of loyalty and am unable to come up with anything".
>
> **Female, 30, Dallas, TX, US**

In fact, as we insist throughout, it is a deep-wired social norm to express only limited interest in products of all sorts. All the really smart Marketing Directors known to Future Foundation always naturally sense that the best intimacies with customers are built on this truth. (As the Baron de Charlus says, it is those who know the limits of friendship who make the best friends). They want those customers to be engaged up to the point of sale and repeat-sale *and no more*. To seek too much enthusiasm, too much *engagement* from shoppers is pure *supply-side* irrationality (which can only beckon *demand-side* rationality, ie the consumer gets irritated or bored or hostile by constant attempts to interest her beyond her natural attitude). A parent might well bring a serious amount of scrutiny down on the choice of Summer mountain camp for the kids but show a step-decline in brand interest when buying emergency aspirin or paper napkins for a children's party or even an online savings account. And what could be more logical?

The smart brand management intuits the level of involvement that really exists from purchase to purchase and from moment to moment. It also assesses just what are the general presumptive impedimenta which consumers might be carrying—social norms, rules of thumb, things people say, what my Mom always told me, stories in the papers, tips from my friends—as they prepare for the moment of choice. And it speaks to them through the creative filter of the **Big Lie**.

What happens when consumers smile at you?

This point made, we might usefully reflect on just how useful in the game of I-Sell-You-Buy are the tools of humor, irony and self-deprecation. Now, of course, it will be true that such tools are sometimes employed because the creative director cannot think of any other idea. Desperation and deadlines drive more brand campaign strategies into play than the cool-headed shortlisting and organized winnowing of all possible plans of attack. But often humor in commercials can be a very pointed if inversed expression of the true, troubled nature of the brand-customer relationship. For frequently the joke will be something of a play on prevailing norms and prejudices. How many TV commercial executions involve playlets which parade the going-wrong of social aspirations or romantic ambitions?

There is, to select just one example, a famous promotion from **Chevrolet** ("Chevy Happy Grad"). This is a short movie in which a young man in a graduation gown mistakenly thinks that his parents have bought him a beautiful yellow convertible. (They have, in fact, bought him a new icebox). His excitement is contrasted with the downbeat faces of his parents who have to wait patiently for him to calm down before releasing the bad news. At the root of the humor lies a riff on the expected, norm-heavy behaviors of doting, middle-class parents who, from before Benjamin Braddock and even since, are programmed to reward academic achievement in suitably, socially ostentatious ways. Elsewhere, how often in the greater culture of TV commercials is fun freely made of gauche lovers, idiotic dads, bumptious authority figures, confused foreigners, people exaggerating their talents or ability to cope in particular situations . . . all rolling around in a comedy of misunderstandings and errors of all sorts? In TV schedules all over the world, it is very easy to find entire programs given over to a mere compilation of fun commercials. Such comedy—making people laugh while trying to sell them stuff or make them think more benevolently about a particular company—is a sub-genre all on its own.

And what does it tell us? It indicates the presence of that very vital but mostly unspoken tension which straddles all market moments. The brand in which the product (a car, a drink, an insurance policy, groceries . . .) is wrapped is speaking to old or potential customers about life's embarrassments and whimsies-gone-wrong *as if all such customers are too smart ever to be the characters in the story.* It is indeed a social norm that human beings are free to laugh at the failures of others without reflecting on the fact that, as they say in Scotland, we are all Jock Tamson's kids, all equally exposed to frailty. To the degree that the kind of advertising executions we reference here show the possibly amusing consequences of *irrational* behavior on the part of consumer-citizens so they, in a way, corroborate the **Big Lie** story. Humor in branding activity is almost invariably part of an attempt to make the viewer feel superior to the dumb guy who does not realize that the beautiful woman is trying to seduce him or the silly over-confident dad who cannot work the barbecue grill without setting fire to his kids' toys. It is thus a means of controlling or moderating the shopper's level of engagement with the product.

To make the viewer chuckle or smile at a commercially purposeful artifact—it is no accident that the ads concerned are often no more than 40 second clips—is to generate a counter-intuitive emotional reaction. There is nothing inherently funny in the business of selling a bottled beer to the youthful male. Our little green Visiting Professor of Earthling Studies would surely find it odd that so many beer commercials make so much fun of earth-male drinking rituals or assumed prejudices (eg that men like to drink beer while evading female company or that beer-drinkers are always making jokes about swearing . . .). No drinking man ever said he likes **Carlsberg** or **Brahma** because he loves the way the commercials thereof make him smile. But in entering the world of that man's social norms to create a humorous conversation, such brands may well contribute to their very continuation, their very value to sales. And besides, humor is a way of lightening and in a sense *de-professionalizing* consumerism; it positively invites a consumer response which has been stripped of any coherent appreciation of a product's intrinsic worth. In a sense, what we discuss here is a stark version of the duplexity of marketing, the means by which a brand can, for example, talk to both a responsible adult and his inner giggly child at the same time.

Why can consumers not just tell everybody what they want?

This leads us, naturally, to reflect on what happens when consumers turn against companies, when there is no laughter but lots of irritability. How does the conversation develop? What social norms form the ropes around the boxing ring? What happens when a brand-owner throws out the rule book, forsakes all sense of propriety and style, breaks for the border? In the UK, people in business still talk about the Ratner Episode. In the early 1990s, a well-known CEO of a jewelry chain, Gerald Ratner, made a speech in which he referred to some of his company's products as *c**p* and suggested that a tuna sandwich might be more valuable than some of the earrings available to shoppers in his stores. The outcry from an insulted public famously led to a disastrous loss of sales and a slump in the stock value of his group.

Now you might well be thinking: what a silly sausage! Of course, his customers reacted badly when he joked so rudely at their expense. But for us the striking thing is just how rare such incidents, such outbursts are within the modern history of consumer-facing business. All good marketing is essentially a language of guileful restraint and qualified respect. If consumers are ever thought to be behaving with a lack of good taste or common sense, then the appropriate thing to say is: nothing. Future Foundation once had a client who was quietly furious that women shoppers never seemed to bother checking the wide range of frozen pizzas that his firm—after much market research and product testing—had made available for in-store sale. Many of the new pizzas, all competitively priced, were very tasty, incorporating many specially requested ingredients and even responding to prevailing nutritional issues and anxieties. But shopper after shopper would pick the same old, same old margherita and walk past the great new gear.

*What was **wrong** with those people?* One had the distinct feeling that if our client had been released onto the aisles, he would have, in his rage and frustration, bought a starfish-shaped, organic Quattro Stagioni with extra truffle oil right down on the head of the next passing Mom. But what to suppliers can seem like an irrational and indeed probably criminal lack of adventure on the part of consumers can be no more than a thoroughly sensible distribution of time and energy to consumers themselves.

The random shopper whom our client would have strangled with one of his own pizzas had maybe once told a focus group that she was bored out of her skull with the drearily predictable choices on offer across the frozen foods departments of her city. So why does she not complete the logic of this position and start buying differently? A conventional answer might be: the market research was inadequately executed and the lady was not really as motivated as the researchers concluded she was. There is within much contemporary marketing scholarship an often-invoked claim that all market research is inherently defective or at best limited in potential value to strategy. Some even go so far as to call it "pseudo-science". Our Future Foundation approach is, once again, anchored in the belief that even though such research may sometimes truly be *limited* it is always *contributory*. It tells us *something*. It feeds the trend narrative, to one degree or another.

There is no such thing as a passive consumer

And while we reflect on this, let us declare that in certain wings of modern marketing guru-lore there is still too much emphasis on the role of the human subconscious—as made out to be some kind of black hole in which the psychological mechanics of choice are busily at work without the individual being aware of the forces driving his or her behavior or being able to direct them through free will.

Such a proposition would, of course, render pretty redundant the whole business of questioning people on their views since individuals cannot, QED, truly know themselves. But positing that consumers are barely aware of why they select a certain suit or washing machine or coffee shop *hardly allows anyone to claim that those consumers are not aware of anything at all*. Besides, one does not need to lean on too many practical examples to realize that the *focus* that a consumer can bring down on a particular choice on a particular day is highly variable.

How many men have just not summoned any energy at all to concentrate on the selection of an engagement ring for the soon-to-be-pleasantly-surprised *namorata*? How many young couples think really deeply about brand selection when buying drinks at the **City Beer Store** for a New Year's Eve party involving 40 college pals all under-thirty? The setting, the importance, the moment, the budget . . . can surely all manage the subconscious to the margins or bring it to the tiller. On other occasions, the pure power of habit—always buying the same style of shoes in the same concession in the same department store—will most assuredly deplete self-awareness and leave the shoe-shopper quite possibly ill-equipped to explain later to a researcher why he bought **Collin Casuals** again today.

The whole argument about the hidden power of the subconscious (leading as it putatively does to all manner of apparent irrationalities on the part of consumers) can get badly over-cooked. Indeed, the argument reminds us of those scholars who tell us things like: *90% (or 60%, whatever) of all communication is non-verbal*. Well, if a man rushes to you in the street shouting *Hey, buddy, your pants are on fire!!!,* you might well presume that the verbal content of the message is going to be pretty dominant for you in that moment. How often it is true that in the elasticity of situations big analytical principles and assertions can get stretched to meaninglessness.

There is a deliciously splenetic seam of commentary in Douglas Rushkoff's book **Present Shock: when everything happens now,** published in 2013. Referencing the modern techniques—as drawn from such disciplines as Behavioral Economics to Neuroscience—which the marketer can notionally employ in pursuit of greater sales and deeper loyalty, he cries out:

*"No matter how invasive the technologies at their disposal, marketers and pollsters never come to terms with the **living process through which people choose** products or candidates; they are looking at what people just bought or thought, and making calculations based on that after-that-fact data. The 'now' they seek to understand tells them nothing about desire, reasons or context. It is simply an effort to key off what we have just done in order to manipulate our decisions in the future".* (Emphasis added).

We make this citation with two thoughts in our ears.

The lesser is that such views confirm and indeed intellectualize some things we say above about the underlying and omnipresent antagonism between shopper and seller. So many moments of sale are the survivors of a great deal of mistrust and suspicion on the part of that shopper and endless effort to persuade ever more effectively on the part of the seller.

The greater is that Rushkoff is absolutely correct to indicate that choice is a dynamic, unstable, *living process* which cannot ever really be captured by any one marketing template, either established or ultra modern. To apply a well-coined trend, however, is to create a space in which the shopper's motives and reactions to stimulus (social, commercial, psychological . . .) can be isolated and weighed.

> "I am loyal to a brand or service as long as they continue to do what made them my first choice. I understand that materials go up and that prices will continue to rise, however if the quality of the brand or service goes down I will choose another that has better quality. I tend to be very loyal, but in this competitive market you have to be consistent. Like the old saying goes, 'What have you done for me today?' You are only as good as your last sale".
>
> **Male, 62, Real Estate Broker, Charlotte, NC, USA**

(For the record, our Future Foundation definition of a trend is: *an empirically observable movement or tendency within prevailing socio-economic conditions which results in a (potentially sustainable) alteration of expectation, decision or behavior on the part of a significant number of citizens and/or institutions*).

Take some trends, season with the Big Lie, bake in a moderate oven for 30 minutes

If our pizza-making client had asked us to address his problem (*innovation overlooked by consumers, their lack of interest and adventurism, a good product going to waste, etc, etc*) and gave us only 30 minutes to present our views, we know what we would have done. It would be essential to talk to him and his team about (given his target demographic) the texture of women's lives, the routines of working Moms, the time-pressures, the need for quick solutions which need not necessarily compromise a craving for something new and different, the health anxieties and agendas, any sense of social conformity (eg the definition of good parenting), all the social norms which condition behavior and constrict self-expression. All this to see which pre-ordained trends would be specially explanatory and strategy-enriching given the business problem at hand.

Trends are envelopes of thought inspired from a judicious and insightful mix of **structural** factors (the things we cannot as individuals change—the economy, income distribution, number of hours in the day, the demographics of the age . . .) and **discretionary** factors (the freedoms we have to choose—where we live, where we take our vacations, what we watch on TV, what we give the kids for dinner . . .).

In any valid and illuminating trend, only the appropriate amount of opinion research will be used. The insight-goal stands still. *Find enough evidence to confirm the story; monitor the trajectory of the trend over time; make an inventory of examples of the trend at work; give advice on the basis of the trend's energy to a particular business sector or brand; accept that the trend's relevance is maybe partial, maybe temporary.* All good insight work is lean and keen. Carries no fat.

Now, the contribution of any opinion research finding to a trend formulation is, initially, a function of its believability or, just as vital, its *un*believability. For example, if around 45% of American women tell our researchers that childcare duties in the home are generally shared, what do we think when around 60% of men tell us the same thing? Around 20% of American men confirm that the spouse is mostly in charge of childcare. This suggests that a lot of sharing is taking place. But around 45% of women say it is mostly them. Both parties cannot be objectively correct in how they are profiling daily life in their answers. Could it be that American men are prone to exaggerating their commitment to domestic duties? Some 30% of US men say that they are generally responsible for food shopping for the family; 4% of American women agree that it is their menfolk who are so responsible. There can hardly be a subject-matter more likely to stimulate responses of the **Big Lie** kind than that of gender relations and the distribution of domestic tasks.

In our notional thirty minutes, we might well talk to our pizza man about some well-established, Future Foundation key trends, auditioning them to see how insightfully they respond to the dynamic of the issue in hand. We might put together a brainstorm pack such as this:

Trend: CHEAP TREATS

. . . *In times and/or regions of low income growth, consumer-citizens are quite capable of creatively re-defining indulgence and fun. And they can readily trade down or across (from one sector to another) in search of luxury. Everyday products (yogurt, shampoo, cookies, pizza . . .) can thus enjoy fantastic re-positioning opportunities that might be hard to sustain in any period of soaring economic growth.*

Trend: ISH!

. . . *No consumer-citizen likes long term contracts any more. No-one likes her customer loyalty to a certain set of products or stores to be assumed and not won—and re-won every day. In the 21st century consumer marketplace, there is no such thing as a pre-nup. Any brand in pursuit of constructive behavioral repetition from customers should probably act as if the kind of innovation which will stimulate interest has to be made ready even before customers realize they might like to change their habits. No matter how long a habit has been in place, the person favoring the same-old, same-old will cut loose any day now.*

Trend: EVERYDAY EXCEPTIONAL

. . . *Insight and innovation have to focus on the business of giving consumers cultural and psychological permission to do something different, break routine, put on a bit of a party hat and share a moment of fun with neighbors, co-workers, family. On any given Tuesday, there must be something to celebrate. This is a trend much energized by social networking and permanent contactability.*

Trend: CULT OF HOME

. . . *The home is now the place where we develop/display our personal accomplishments perhaps even more than we do at work. Nobody boasts or laughs about being a hopeless under-achiever any more. The home is the focus and the platform for so much super-smart living, the place where waste is minimized, nutrition maximized, economies relentlessly pursued, casual togetherness cherished.*

Trend: HEALTHY HEDONISM

. . . The invitation to all Americans to take personal care of their health and specially their weight has never been more socially or politically insistent. And never has there been so much precise scientific advice about what is good for us and in what proportions. This imposes a discipline on consumer-citizens which is hard to sustain in every moment of the day. To the extent that we still crave luxurious indulgence, products can meet the need by offering the old, unchanged, full-fat experience (Go on—one jelly doughnut will not kill you) or by making healthy products somehow luxurious or by re-defining indulgence in terms of an extra health kick (via super-functional foods).

Now, the goal in such an endeavor is to explore how such a mix of (non-exhaustive) trends—interacting and overlapping as they do—might inspire new ways to communicate with so far under-motivated shoppers while checking, point by point, the effectiveness of current strategy. Perhaps it will be true that the pizza brand can exert only a moderate influence over issues such as store layout or a feature such as the times of the week or day when most of the target shoppers head downtown in search of family meals. But to the extent that the brand can talk directly to its supporters and invent the products that they might require then such trends analysis can—and this is the heart of the story—suggest which buttons do not need to be pushed or pushed quite so much. No trend should ever act as if consumers are more interesting than they are. Every trend is rendered valid by how well it discloses the true weight of consumer motives and moods. This is why our **Big Lie** proposition is usefully applied as a filtering device.

We can take a simple example. Less than 20% of American women tell our researchers that they but *rarely* check food labels to find out how healthy the product is. Well, how many Moms are going to admit that they are so rushed from day to day and so reliant on repeat purchases from familiar companies that they do not take active steps to verify that they are buying healthy foods for the family? Should supplying brands, in their dialogue with shoppers, *act as if* labels are regularly and thoroughly checked? Yes, they should. It would be disrespectful not to do so. (If Grandma Jenny tells a story from the old days, one that you have heard twenty times before, is it not proper or polite to smile and nod as you hear it one more time?).

Moreover, our research also shows that when American women are asked whether they are interested in labeling which clearly illuminates the health qualities of a product *then 80% are not in the Strongly Agree category.* When asked about their actual behavior, perhaps many of our respondents are ready to say something that corresponds to what would be expected by others (given, for example, their perceived leadership role as homemakers and mothers). When asked, implicitly, about how much extra energy they would like to expend on scrutinizing and checking the food that is bought for the home, then the responses droop. This we would not find surprising. The social norm effect is not quite as strong when respondents are asked to speculate and hypothesize rather than represent their own day to day behavior.

It may well be that the outcome of the trends-sifting process we outline above is a conclusion that the process of product innovation is running too far ahead of the customer's ability to absorb. Perhaps the appetite for new textures and flavors is, whatever is said out loud, pretty shallow. Perhaps something needs to be done to try to alter the perception of the product category rather than an individual brand. Maybe the new pizzas are not being associated in the shopper's mind with her own self-perceived skills—their ability to make the banal turn into something special, the repetitive mealtime behavior into something fresh and creative. One way or another, it has to be assessed whether any market failing—product being left on the shelf—is the consequence of a) under-activated trends analysis and/or b) too much of an un-nuanced response to what people say (and think it best to say) in opinion research exercises.

The **Big Lie** theory and all that goes with it does not guarantee commercial success. But it should put into measured juxtaposition a dispassionate appreciation of how people actually live inside their heads *and* the generalized assumptions made by both people themselves and by those who bring things to market. It may be that trends analysis does nothing more than take away a lot of mental clutter from proceedings. It may be that it helps locate a different source of a particular problem (wrong pricing model, under-performing packaging, poor quality ingredients . . .). And it may well also be that one well-worked trend identifies the space in which competitive advantage can be won and sustained. One way or another, listening to the consumer's inner voice and searching for the real reasons why they do the sometimes funny things they do is both a wisdom and a humanism. No brand can fail to draw benefit from such a process.

Let's finally imagine a group of baseball fans who visit a particular coffee stand on their way to and from the stadium. Asked why they stop there, they predominantly tick *wide range of regular and de-caffeinated choices*. But casual empiricism + sales figures show that they mostly all drink a tall Americano at every visit. Should the owner, planning to establish more stands around the stadium, conclude that she should a) maintain or even increase the product range at all her venues in the light of the findings b) save money by *minimizing* the product range on offer because there is something holding her market in place which her consumers either are not themselves realizing or are not acknowledging? Or some variant on the two questions? (They like her serving staff? One dominant individual likes the stand and his buddies follow? The general habit is so embedded that the customers themselves no longer know why they still go there? It is a very handy venue but, given the questions put by the nice market research person, they want—at some level—to *intellectualize* their behaviors?).

Observation and interrogation on the part of coffee stand owners, pizza producers and brand managers in general rarely combine to produce instantaneous and fully elegant answers to questions of human motive. And as every politician knows, successfully inducing behavioral change among citizens—even when their interests provably lie in a particular direction—is almost never a question of yanking the most obvious levers. But the logic of prevailing choice or continuing habit or apparently foolish inertia is always buried somewhere and can therefore always be unearthed. In all such endeavors, the **Big Lie** proposition might well direct you to the trends which will help you the most.

Intuitions for Insight

- For as long as we all live in a marketplace of adversarialism—*me* consumer, *you* brand—it will be in the natural order of things for marketplace conversations to be populated by half-truths, disguised feelings, oblique remarks.
- Just as brand-owners recognize this, so they also stay alert to the appearance of self-deceiving comments from consumers or statements which bear the imprint of social expectations. It is under the umbrella of the **Big Lie** that all opinion research findings have to read.
- Some amount, some *quality* of rationality is to be found in every consumer action. Too much enthusiasm on the part of the consumer is very definitely a form of irrationality and brands should not encourage it.
- But, even if insight can locate the logic that is there, it does not follow that either brand communications or new product invention should directly address or make an appeal to that logic. The most valuable thing a brand-owner can do is to storyboard what might really be transpiring in consumers' heads as they approach the moment of purchase. Sometimes segmenting (in the old-fashioned way) by consumer *type* may be less revealing than segmenting by the precepts of the **Big Lie**: the identification of multiple and quite possibly unstable motives.

- The best brands cock their ear to the customer's inner monologue while knowing that what is said out loud by that same person may well be partial but will be endlessly revealing evidence.
- The **Big Lie** proposition prompts all brands to ask: what is really holding our sales figures in place and how, accepting that it may be different tomorrow to what it was yesterday, do we influence it in our long-term interests? This is a good daily question for every conceivable consumer-facing sector.

CHAPTER TWO

POWER OF ME, VALUE OF WE

Questions for Analysis

- How much open acknowledgement of group influence in their lives are consumer-citizens now ready to make?
- In brand business, an enormous amount of analytical effort is directed at the question: why do our customers choose what they choose? Is there a sound and successful way of separating group influence from genuinely independent personal choice? And is such a distinction, such a task really meaningful?
- Consumers seem to be getting smarter. Does this mean they need less support to make good decisions?

- If we all require less formal social endorsement of our lifestyle choices, do we grow more confident in our ability, as private consumers, to optimize our decisions?
- Does technological innovation herald the de-casualization of influence via the power of smart systems, easily triggered at every moment of marketplace choice?
- At the heart of human motive and appetite, are there indeed universal and permanent truths which insight must always respect?

Consumer brainpower: hard to deny, hard to measure

There are some prominent analysts of consumer behavior who in their books and reports make much of the dark power of the human subconscious. They make a lot of noise about the hidden unknowable forces inside our hidden unknowable selves—forces which defy any commonplace claim that rational choice is present in what we do as consumers when we set out to buy things. Self-awareness becomes, in this scheme of things, something of a delusion.

OK. Consider this.

Your teenage daughter has a headache, a terrible headache. You drive down to the pharmacy to ask for advice. While you are waiting, you Google "Adolescent Headaches" and start to wonder, on the basis of what you read on various sites and blogs, whether Vanessa has recently been spending too much time in front of a screen. You then talk to the nice man in the white coat but something in his manner suggests to you that he is not really confident in what he is saying. He is giving too much semaphore: . . . *on the one hand, on the other hand, on the next hand . . . it could be . . .* Just then, your wife texts you to hurry; Vanessa is lying like a python on the sofa.

You make a quick scan of the analgesics on the shelves and select a brand which, you recall, your wife herself has used in the past and which proved effective.

Now, at what point in this process, did you—our notional consumer—behave *irrationally*? In what moments were you in the grip of subcutaneous forces that, though you could not feel them, were dictating your reactions?

Hold the questioning. Let's take another example.

In this case, you are another person.

This Sunday, it's your boyfriend's birthday. You have been going out for three months and you could not be more sold on him. He likes Italian. So, even though you yourself know more than a few good places, you check **Yelp** for the best dinner venue and reserve a corner table. You know only a little about champagne and so you ask some pals for guidance and as a result you leave a bottle of **Krug** by his games-console for him to find that morning. It's expensive bubbles. But precisely because it is not an everyday brand he will appreciate all the more the focused affection behind the gift. You mean these presents to mean business. And they do. And for the dinner date you wear new **Kasil** jeans, favored by so many movie stars.

Anything *not-thought-through* in any of this? Any automaton-esque behavior?

If either of our two notional people were questioned by market researchers after these events, could those researchers discover, though diligent questioning, why they had done what they had done, chosen what they had chosen?

On what basis did our people sometimes rely on their own judgement and sometimes judiciously draw wisdom from the experience of others?

How much did it matter that these were moments when it was vital to get things right? Could this be uncovered and appreciated by outsiders to the story? Was the pre-ordained fame of particular brands a helpful shortcut at any point? What would our shoppers themselves agree or admit was true about their behavior?

> "I find it important to have my own views on issues and have my own tastes, as I don't like to think that I just follow the crowd and want to have my own mind and come to conclusions about things independently".
>
> **Female, 27, London, UK**

Well, maybe researchers would struggle to unravel the full narrative here in each case. Imagine that some general qual or quant questions were put (some three months after each incident described) to each individual, questions about sources of advice, the role of established brands in driving choice, the importance of following what others normally do . . .

Generalized responses would perhaps disguise the weight of such things in particular situations. Respondents might elevate their own discretion, their own knowledge. The **Big Lie** might well rear. But that would not mean there was no logic at work in each sequence of attitudes and behaviors. In the end, moreover, it might well be not remotely interesting to discuss any obscure subconscious forces, whether they were really at work in all this or not. Sometimes contributors (to this kind of motive-exploration) talk of the subconscious as if it were a desert island that contains a treasure-chest of deep truths to explain everything—and they, as consultants, might just be able to prise it open for you, their client. But human reality can sometimes be ordinary and discoverable. *In extremis,* for example, *veritas.*

We hold these questions electric in our head as we proceed now to address a vital **Big Lie** issue. To what degree can any one person, whatever he or she thinks or says, truly act *alone*? When a private decision is taken, no matter how slight the subject, is a crowd of some kind always in the room? As the 21st century progresses, does a richer economy mean that more of us can successfully individuate ourselves away from the herd? Or is the urge to conform as secretly robust as ever? And does that urge still solve many day to day problems for us? *I do not know what to pick here . . . They seem to know what to pick here . . . I will pick here what they pick here.*

The crowd gets smarter—and so do I

Very few people run their own church, a religion only for themselves. Few completely abjure family life. The occupation of solitary lighthouse keeper is not popular. There is no sight sadder than that rare funeral with no mourners. People who need people, as the old song runs, are the luckiest people in the world.

Now, a standard and well-trod narrative, available in all good business bookshops, here would be this.

As incomes rise and household wealth accumulates—something of an ironic intro, we freely accept, given the experience of many families in the Western world in this decade—so individuals grow in confidence. In such conditions, they can depend less on collectivist institutions and pre-cooked doctrines or respectabilities to live successfully. For they can afford to make the odd mistake, break a convention here and there and then decide, in the light of outcomes, whether the convention was ever one worth following or not.

Let's look into this.

As time has passed, it is certainly true that Americans, Europeans and many others have become better educated and thus more empowered to investigate and weigh the choices they have to make. They can more readily probe the suggestions that others make for them and even resist the pressures put on them to share a much-shared point of view.

As it is going to become even more relevant to this argument later, let's linger on some numbers for a second here. In the US, there are around 3.4 million young people graduating high school each year—that is 80% of the population of 17 year olds. In 2000, the figure was less than 70% and in the late 40s less than 60%. Soon, there will be over 2 million BA degrees granted each year; in 1981, there were around 950,000 BAs granted. Now, we pick this touch-point year because this was the last year in America when, so tellingly, women took *fewer* degrees than men. (Source: **US Census Bureau**). In the UK, there are now 2.5 times as many people receiving degrees as there were a generation ago. (Source: **National Statistics UK**). The proportion of pupils in England gaining 5 GCSEs is now around 80% and was but 50% at the start of the century. (Source: **House of Commons**). The proportion of Australians who hold a qualification achieved post-school rose from just less than 50% in 2000 to ca 60% by 2012. (Source: **ABS**). In Germany, some 45% of those aged 25 to 35 now hold a qualification in the *Fachhochschulreife/Hochschulreife* (ie university level) category—compared to around a quarter of that same generation's parents. (Source: **Destatis**).

It is hard to think of a country, outside North Korea or those parts of Asia/Africa disfigured by war and civil disorder, where the scale of educational attainment is not both spreading and deepening. We hold it to be a self-evident (and under-appreciated) truth that this is *such* a dynamic element in the forward march of civilization itself, never mind markets. Any static, retrospective, true-for-all-time maxim about consumer behavior—and, yessir, there are plenty of those out there, still searching for repeat custom in the world of trends consultancy—is by definition not respectful of this very truth.

Once upon a time, **Death of a Salesman** was a great play, powerfully explanatory of its era and the sadnesses which could inhabit it. Once, Punk was the very edge of edge. Once, blue-haired Blake Carrington ran the fantasy **Dynasty** into which the American Dream had turned. Then came Gordon Gekko and Jane Fonda and her work-outs while the Cold War disappeared and while, in so many places, the old smokestack industries disappeared too—just as the Human Genome and GMOs drove the purposeful application of modern science in the lives of billions. Francis Fukuyama put an end to history while gangsta rap put an end to the silence of the disaffected, inner-city male. Then the internet came along to change everything—communicating, having fun, building knowledge. It is just unimaginable that those living through any of the above are not aware that much can be shifted and shed from decade to decade—including and especially the role of norms and tribes in the lives of everyman and everywoman.

The same kind of movements and vibrations are so eminently detectable in the world of satisfying human need by the provision of goods. Once, a strategy for bringing a new idea to the cosmetics counter or the toy store could be based on them old Three Ps of Marketing. Then some companies, dressed in T-shirts, thought about taking the super-highway to market and shooting past the lazy bus-full of men in boring white shirts carrying all those nonagenarian assumptions about what a business model is. Meanwhile, Moore's Law affirmed the inevitable squaring and re-squaring of processing power. Many of us stopped going to the shops to buy books and movies and newspapers and even clothes. We started selling our old dresses to strangers, joining buying groups to drive down the cost of heating oil, ordering our groceries by tapping on a technicolor handheld screen.

But, all along this road too, consumer-audiences (it is prudent to assume) get smart, see the join, need new jokes. What was once a usefully heuristic herd behavior to your Dad is bafflingly shallow to your teenage daughter. Any glance at TV commercials from the 1950s will reveal a communications language which today would be understood as well as Navajo wind-talking. Insight cannot rest on eternal truths. It should look for what is changing. Adjust to what is working. And assume that the audience is not permanently at the mercy of dark forces that they cannot alter. All such insight should beware of any claim that there are anthropological certainties forever governing life.

Social values: slackening and tightening at the same time

Back to the skilling of the 21st century consumer. Of course, there is a running hubbub of complaint that school tests are easier these days, that the old intellectual disciplines are not imposed like they used to be, that qualifications are bestowed too liberally. You never see a headline in a newspaper: *National education—best it's ever been!* But let us insist on our point here. Whenever any market opens in the morning—the local butcher, the department store, the bank downtown, all the online auction sites, **Wallgreens** and **Amazon**, **McDonald's** and **Ticketmaster**—the generation of customers who walks through will be formally smarter than any that has gone before. This is a function not just of their school record but also, of course, of their easy access to a scale of information about price and quality which was simply not available to their grandparents.

In his book, **The Better Angels of Our Nature**, Steven Pinker makes much of what is known as the Flynn Effect. This is a reference to the work of James Flynn who revealed some years ago that human IQ scores seem to be, controlling for all that needs to be controlled, *improving* as the decades pass.

"Flynn suggests that over the course of the 20th century, scientific reasoning infiltrated from the schoolhouse and other institutions into everyday thinking. More people worked in offices and the professions where they manipulate symbols rather than crops, animals and machines. People had more time for leisure and they spent it in reading, playing combinatorial games and keeping up with the world".

We so need to keep in mind this evolutionary dimension in the field of consumer tracking; its very stark implication is that people's approach to problem-solving + opportunity-maximizing can indeed sharpen. And *the role of group norms therein* may a) not be static over time or b) may well find new forms of commercially interesting expression. The **Big Lie** does not, one imagines, fossilize; it adjusts to its environment and breeds in new places.

Meanwhile, it is also true that many social rules have been relaxed to allow greater individual discretion. The marriage vows are not, in many cases, the *till-death-do-us-part* contractual obligations they used to be. In many places, gay people can join together in civil arrangements or even marriage to an extent unimaginable a generation ago. Cohabitation is a frequently acceptable form of either intimacy-experiment or intimacy-settlement. The **US Census Bureau** informs that in the first decade of this century the number of households containing an unmarried couple increased by a thumping 40% while the rate of divorce has been falling, presumably as a consequence. (Broken cohabitations are not regularly recorded in official statistics). The incidence of cohabitation in the UK doubled, **National Statistics** says, in the period 1996 to 2012. In France, according to **Insée,** around a third of living-together couples are not married.

Amid this, there are fewer hand-me-down uniforms these days. Just because your father runs a hardware store then this is no reason for you to do the same. You do not need to support **the Boston Red Sox** just because your family has always done so; for from your home in Ashmont you might well actually prefer spending your Sundays playing online with your **Gameknot** chess team-buddies in San Francisco. Your baseball-mad family teases you about this. But you do not care. The tribal writ does not run so hard these days.

More, you might well want to live in the same town where you were born but this is principally a matter of choice these days. If you like wearing an open-necked, checked shirt to your office (while the co-worker next to you wears a suit and tie) or a pair of jeans in an upscale trattoria, then it is highly likely that nobody will look critically or huffily at you. There are relatively fewer places in life where you will be told: *that is just not done.*

The whole crowd can inhabit one individual

The funny thing is this. Individualism becomes, paradoxically for the trends analyst, something of a collective ideal. For the supremacy of individual choice is the major dynamo of the market economy.

In so many market situations, this is the one-size-fits-nobody generation. Now, of course, there are markets which try to prosper by controlling and indeed compressing the possibilities for individuated service. Low-cost air travel would be an example. And your local plumber cannot fix your broken faucet in either a standard or a premium or deluxe way. But so much *offer* is now programmed to allow consumers to select from a scale or a range—from the duvet weight in an hotel room to the number of movie channels in a TV package to the colors and textures in your jogging shoes.

(As we write, the **Reebok** website boasts around 3.5 million "unique designs and counting". The **NikeiD** pages allow you to customize your shoes across a total number of variations it would take a math professor to calculate. **Adidas** invites its soccer fans: "Like David Beckham, Customize your Boot").

Obviously, we are not referencing here acts of blind commercial humanitarianism. It can seriously profit companies to create new and indeed multiple price points and thus maximize revenues and repeat business. It is not all about giving shoppers more fun or being more, as so many vapid marketing guidebooks insist on saying, customer-centric. But the effect of such practices is to bestow and reinforce the shopper's sense of personal importance, a feeling of being in charge, that confirmation that what she (and nobody else) thinks matters a very great deal.

The story, however, has its social twists and psychological turns. Very few of us ever say to friends over tennis-club drinks: *You know, I really prefer to wear the style of party shoes that everyone else seems to be wearing.* It just sounds somehow wrong to say out loud: *The real reason I buy this detergent is because my Mom used to buy it.*

Or: *I admire that Congressman because he is often on television and seems to be popular with a lot of people in my circle.*

So many of us consider ourselves as what used to be called "inner-directed", coolly able to scrutinize life-choices, masters and mistresses of all decisions, frivolous and profound. And so, along the way, the climate for expressions of the **Big Lie** is much favored. The cult of individualism means never having to say: *Actually, a lot of the time I just do what everyone else does.*

> "I believe people want to believe their life is more exciting and less restricted and posting photos and creating a more upbeat online persona helps them. Everyone acts differently at work, at their home with family, so it's understandable that people create a character online".
>
> **Female, 29, NYC, USA**

This is not to deny the very obvious importance of what, used loosely, is called *self-actualizing*. Our internet generation has indeed seen an explosion in opportunities for personal creativity through planned consumption and shared experience. Millions post movie reviews, recipes, carpentry tips. At least some of us can take vacations in places where few tourists go, beating our own path into the jungle or up the mountains. One can select a fusion of soft furnishing styles for the home and not be ridiculed by friends but rather admired for some adventurous, convention-challenging tastes. Novelists do not any more write stories nor songwriters songs about the stifling imprisonment of über-uniformed suburban life. No Richard Yates, no **Revolutionary Road**, no Pete Seeger, no **Little Boxes** made of Ticky Tacky. Nobody says to **The Graduate** *de nos jours*: "Just one word. Plastics!". There is just no space left, so it would seem, for an **Abigail's Party** or a **Semi-Detached Suburban Mr. James**.

There can often be a heavy moralistic overhang to this debate. There are those who see damage being done in any flourishing of individualism. For it may lead to perverted introspection, a turning away from the important rituals of family life, a decline in neighborliness and general insensitivity to the legitimate agendas of others in our community, a solipsistic devotion to solitary and often screen-based leisure . . .

The social devaluation of the solitary cyclist

Perhaps the most famous version of this strain of argument was **Bowling Alone**, Robert Putnam's book of 2000. He spoke of a "sense of civic malaise" and sought to measure various manifestations of what he saw as weakened social engagement and depleted social capital. The interesting thing for us here is that this is one of many sociological treatises which—whatever the objective truth of what they report—echo a sometimes unspoken but often quite tangible assumption that too much individualism has to be, well, a bad thing. It is as if it is associated with a natural swelling of unpleasant, self-absorbent vanity or the kind of isolation that threatens psychological wellbeing.

Nobody running for senior political office will put on her campaign literature that she is not really interested in family life, has never spoken much to the others who live on her block, rather dislikes the district where she is running—even though all of that is true. Good fences make good neighbors, as Robert Frost once told us. But in day to day living, friendly and matey people are generally regarded as probably safe and sane. No doubt there is a scholarly book somewhere which concludes that that the old Marquis de Sade invented S&M just because he was stuck in a cell in the Bastille for rather too long for his own good. Seriously too much self-actualizing there.

Now it does indeed seem to be true that flamboyantly individualistic people tend not to be socially favored.

Yes, there is a measure of cultural freedom given to an Angelina Jolie or a Dennis Rodman or a Silvio Berlusconi or a Lindsay Lohan . . . But most of us like to go to work and run our homes surrounded by calm, predictable people who broadly, whatever the situation, behave the way we do. When that woman at the barbecue, to whom you had just been introduced, started whispering to you about her acrobatic sex life without even taking the cigar out of her mouth, you somehow knew it was time to split. A good assumption is that the more other persons are like us then—celebrities apart—the more we will be influenced by them. We are programmed to shun excessive displays of ego or eccentricity.

> "I really don't like to be recognized or known by others, as I like to remain quite unnoticed. I don't like those kinds of people who continually have to be flattered by others, because, from my point of view, this clearly indicates a strong insecurity".
>
> **Female, 25-34, student, social networker, Spain**

But nonetheless, most people, we freely hazard, feel generally strong in their choice-making ability, seeing themselves as individuals who can handle things, sift the messages emitted in TV commercials or by in-store sales assistants, move through life not easily manipulated or duped. In 2010, Future Foundation asked people around the world to respond to the statement: *I usually pay attention to television advertising.* Only 5% agreed strongly in the US, 3% in the UK, hardly a living soul in Scandinavia. Interruption marketing, so-called, has had something of a bad press among insight professionals over the last decade (perhaps ever since Seth Godin's **Permission Marketing** of 1999). It gets an even worse press among consumers themselves. Or so they say.

Of course, the number of books written about the true role of external influences in the lives of consumers could, laid end to end, fill an entire waste recycling facility. (And, though the point will not detain us here, it is striking how often trends analysts are influenced by what they read in books about, well, theories of influence). But we turn now to what would be generally taken to be the—always a potential oxymoron in the making—conventional wisdom about the role of crowd-influence and herd-behavior in the daily doings of consumers everywhere.

Study after scholarly study parades examples of ordinary, well educated consumers choosing a meal in a restaurant or a music download or even stock in which to invest the family savings . . . *exclusively* on the basis of what appears to be popular with others who have previously done the choosing and left helpful messages to new consumers to read or examples to follow. The fact that there is much reluctance on the part of consumers to admit that this at least might be true (and that they are indeed heavily influenced accordingly) could be thought to be one of the most obvious manifestations of the **Big Lie** in captivity.

The whole psychology of collective influence, in all its modern sophistications, has much energized the praxis of Behavioral Economics. This is especially true in its public policy applications, such as prevailing on people to conserve energy in the home, look after the countryside better when they go visiting, donate blood and organs to those who need them, etc, etc. How striking it is that so much of the messaging which would trace its origins to the hallowed precepts of BE involves telling people that, from situation to situation, they would be better off following the majoritarian view. (Of course, we accept that BE can be used to beckon people to behave badly on exactly the same principle. But this does not really deflect our point and will not detain us here).

In the UK, for one example, the "Nudge Unit" of Her Majesty's Government's Cabinet Office has made much of the fact that it can engineer an increase in the tax-take by communicating to potential miscreants that most of their neighbors are paying their taxes on time. And it will be something of an exhausted cliché to mention again that marketing and advertising tradespeople have long since understood the value of proposing their products to shoppers by stressing that *many-other-folks-just-like-you* are buying this car insurance, that bottled beer, this newspaper, that air freshener. If the Creative Director cannot think of a new twist to the campaign, then she can always use this for the execution: *Eight out of ten women prefer it.* It is an old trick. But it might just work.

One very much doubts, though, that were wannabe tax evaders in the English provinces to be asked *why* they had kept to the payment deadline they would say: *Well, actually mate, I did in the end think it best to stick to the group norms on this subject, the norms which do seem to be prevalent in and around Greater Manchester at the current time.* No more than a young woman in San Francisco would fail to say out loud that she buys, say, **Revlon Colorsilk** for her hair because of the intrinsic qualities of the product. Nothing to do with the fact that it is a popular brand and, by the way, the beautiful Olivia Wilde endorses it.

For a while there, Behavioral Economics seemed like something new and revolutionary, a surefire scheme by which to detonate massive changes in the conduct of consumer-citizens. But really a lot of BE simply re-discovers things learned in the advertising business long before even **Sterling Cooper** opened for business. Perhaps the biggest continually re-learned message is that the individual simply likes to be reassured that a decision taken at the shops involves the minimum of risk—risk defined as making a faux pas, going out on a pointless limb, exposing oneself to even the slightest ridicule or just finding oneself with a bad deal. In contemporary marketing literature, much is made of the eruption of neuroscience into this ever evolving narrative of social influencing. Much is especially made of the power of **Functional Magnetic Resonance Imaging** to track brain activity, blood flows, general responses to external situational stimulus . . . And the suggestion from related research is that a) people feel better when they go with the group choice in a specific circumstance—ie herd-following has an almost *narcotic* effect— and that b) their own powers of discretionary decision-taking are distorted when a strong group preference is being voiced around them. Is this not the very Higgs-Boson of the **Big Lie**?

The irony burning at the heart of self-actualization

We suspend our broadcast at this junction to introduce a well-established Future Foundation trend, something tracked around the globe over many years: **Personalization of Authority**. Put simply, this is the story of how we bend less to authority figures, we resist social imperatives when they fail to suit us, we can cut our own deals in life. In fact, we all can gather what some still loosely call social capital by parading our own independently developed *savoir-vivre*, *savoir-faire*, and, of course, *savoir-acheter*. Rather than bowling alone we are bowling intelligently—in creative interaction with socio-economic conditions much different to those faced by our grandparents.

What breaks into view is this question: are the times we inhabit more propitious to the *power of me* (as we are discussing it here) or is collectivized influence even more energized by the realities of our ever modernizing, digital world? Could it be that, under different pressures and moments, the answer to both questions is positive? And precisely what does the filter of the **Big Lie** proposition allow us to learn about future shifts in consumer behavior?

It seems like a dollar-store platitude as one says it out loud but the **Digital Revolution** has done an immeasurable amount to increase consumer-citizen empowerment and, on the surface at least, to deplete any dependency on groups or tribes or socio-cultural inheritances of any kind. Consider the availability of what we might call wisdom-retrieval. If you suddenly fancy catching an old Meg Ryan movie, your friendly online retailer might, before you click, alert you to the fact that you actually bought **Proof of Life** back in 2002. You have a dispute with a boss who, after he has promoted your sycophantic colleague to the VP role that you should have won, claims you never told him that you had a degree in statistics; but you are able to disinter the inculpatory email from 2007. You are not certain that your new doctor is offering a correct treatment for your recurrent breathing difficulties; but you are able to draw down from your specialist cloud-source supplier the entire documentary history of your medical consultations; this gives you decisive intelligence for your dealings with her. So far, so everyday. So many situations occur where we can ignite all kinds of personal intelligence, about matters small and great, in our favor.

Now, in theory, this should lead to a much weakened interest in alternative opinion, the comfort of strangers, the wisdom of crowds. Personalized authority stands tall, no?

But here we must factor another realism of the 21st century: *the volume of human decision-making activity massively exceeds the human capacity to efficiently process every choice.*

If you think we exaggerate, consider the hegemony of habit in our lives. Functional routines—eg driving to the same supermarket every Saturday morning, staying with the same dentist, buying the latest John Grisham (your usual favorite)—which have the effect of blocking any rational discussion of whether such products/ services are offering consistent value-for-money are as empirically potent in our days as ever. Many sectors—arguably, for instance, personal banking and insurance—depend deeply on the customer's unwillingness to find the energy to scrutinize the products they buy year in and year out—even when, incidentally, there may well be a clamor of good advice from experts and friends alike to shop for better deals. The *Value of We* has its strange limits.

Sometimes in this debate it's not a question of the ever smarter consumer-citizen being able to work out, on her own, what are the best things to do/the best things to buy; it's a question of *why* she does not process the good advice that might well be echoing round her tribe. One has only to think of the decades spent by public policy campaigners trying to get us all to stop smoking, to eat fruit rather than ribs, to take simple lifestyle precautions against inter-personal infections . . . Sometimes group influence can be significant for its very *lack* of influence. All those dogs barking in the garden—yet Jack and Lisa still do not get off the sofa. Not so much **Big Lie** as Big Lazy.

Meanwhile, how often do those in the marketing trades ever identify a truly alpha-consumer segment—those able to know everything about, say, desktop printers for home use? Well, there will always be some super-nerdy people who will fall into this category. But will those same people still perform as dominant consumers as they move from printers to vitamin supplements to vacations in Costa Rica to appropriate fantasy novels for a fourteen year old daughter? Very unlikely. There is a limit, once more, to what we actually want to prioritize and to process.

This naturally becomes a discussion about all the decisions to be taken regularly now, decisions that barely troubled us, if at all, a generation ago. Which cell phone contract to select from the hundreds of options and packages available? When to upgrade both our smartphone and our tablet—and which features to prioritize in our daily usage? How to assess the differential qualities of Blu-Ray and HD TV? How to organize your son's year of back-packing in Vietnam before he starts at MIT? Which pension plan to buy? How to use apps to help ensure that we are getting a balanced diet and taking precisely the correct amount of cardiovascular exercise? How to apply online for welfare? How much to spend on a GPS? How to work our TV systems so that commercial breaks are skipped and all the episodes of **The Real Housewives of New Jersey** and **How to Live with Your Parents (For the Rest of Your Life)** are saved for later viewing . . . ?

Being a 21st century consumer can be a hard day's night.

So much technological innovation beckons us into markets we never knew we needed. So much free delivery of advice and guidance. So much conventional but still very inventive advertising on our radio stations and on the colorful auto-looped billboards on the way to work. So many alternative options for you—among all the books, DVDs, audio tapes, classes, concierge services—as you reflect on the best way to manage a naughty child or cook a turkey at Thanksgiving or Christmas. Back in the late 1990s, it was commonly thought that the internet was going to turn into nothing more than a huge sluice of human unpleasantness, notably a portal for the most lurid pornography. Nobody but nobody predicted it would all soon come with a free encyclopedia, not just for knowledge but for living and with free, dispassionate advice about how to improve every aspect of one's day. If this is the age of Big Data it is also the age of Mega-Multiple Choice. And, let's be honest, one of complicated lives. Yes, we may well all be smarter (as reviewed earlier). But we have more work to do. And perhaps there is a limit to how much efficiency we can muster from day to day.

More, there are so many socially reinforced invitations to personal accomplishment these days. There are just so many TV shows which show you how to cook proper paella or how to lose weight from your thighs or how to plan the perfect wedding; so many self-help books and you-can-change-your-looks/career/lovelife/garden/hair/shape/ doctor . . . features in magazines. Nobody thinks that the klutz is amusing any more. At the dinner party of 21st century life, the person who brags to fellow guests about knowing nothing about wine is silently pitied. Perhaps once it was groovy to float loftily above the trails of a tawdry consumerism. But there is no audience for this kind of attitude, this special kind of 20th century **Big Lie**, any more.

> "The reason I update things on Facebook is simply to keep in touch—never to show off, although I admit to posting provoking comments when an important issue is at stake".
>
> **Female, 55+, music-lover, Madrid, Spain**

As you go to click "Purchase", who is really in charge?

One does not need to be an evolutionary psychologist or path-breaking neuroscientist to know and to notice that all of life, as lived now in the way we describe, is an exercise in summary and *often inelegantly* applied summary. Even those with a particularly deep sense of **Personalized Authority** have to take shortcuts, guess the right route quickly, depend on half-digested tips. It is fascinating to explore just how consumer-citizens feel about talking about this reality. When Future Foundation puts to its sample of US citizens a proposition like: *If a friend or a family member recommends a product or service to me I am much more likely to buy it* then around 60% will be ready to agree. (A similar response is, incidentally, found in other mature consumer markets such as the EU). This seems normal enough in the sense that a) one may well have a high enough level of trust in, for example, one's circle of college friends to recommend great new bars and coffee shops and b) in responding positively to this particular statement one is not sounding like just a plaything of wide, sweeping social opinions. It is somehow *OK* to admit influence from *your* family and the people you have chosen to be *your* friends.

> "The only people that I care to be recognized by are my family. It is the only opinion that I really care about. It is nice to be recognized by peers, friends and associates but this is not what is important to me".
>
> **Male, 62, real estate broker, grandfather, Charlotte, NC, USA**

What opens here is, of course, a psychological reality of significant value to all those brands trying constantly to build better communications and tighter intimacies with customers. As all the survey findings are investigated here, one notices also that it can be around 30% of respondents who *neither agree nor disagree* with the proposition. Such a proportion and such a response should indeed interest the insight professional. The question is whether such respondents are genuinely never influenced by family and friends *or* whether they are uncertain about being so influenced *or* whether they would feel somehow *impeded from confirming* to a stranger that they are so influenced. It is the latter which would form our own working assumption here. Now, of course, situational reality can matter a whole lot more than generalized attitude for such a story. A man may well not want to admit to his wife that he really bought a **Honda Fit** as the new family car because he much admired the nice saleslady—*name of Jenna, wants to be an actress*—at the showroom or because his best friend was thinking about buying the same car. Nobody ever says he bought a particular big ticket item because the promotional TV commercials were really good.

When Future Foundation puts forth a quantitative proposition such as: *A well-known brand—eg* **Coca Cola**, **Toyota**, **Samsung**, **Visa**—*is the best assurance of quality there is*, then less than 30% of respondents in, again, mature markets such as the US and the UK will corroborate. Meanwhile, in those *still-getting-used-to-wealth* countries such as China and India, there will be a *majority* of middle-class citizens who agree. Though we would never dare to build a working model of global consumerism from a solitary piece of survey data, we have good grounds for believing that in the major emerging markets it is not a mark of social de-sophistication to love what others love, crave what others have. From the Future Foundation quant archives, we know that it is about 60% of our Indian sample who agree that: *I like other people to be able to recognize the brands I wear*; the equivalent figure for a market like Sweden is less than 10%.

Hearing the herd the 21st century way . . .

We put our point another way.

In Western societies, it is precisely a consequence of heightened individualism that it becomes harder to admit to being too much influenced by others.

In his book **The Power of Habit**, Charles Duhigg builds a useful narrative about how what masquerades as rational choice is often little more than embedded repetition. This is presumably as much true for the smartest in our midst as it is for the dreamiest. At one point, referencing sources of influence in favor of either established habits or new behaviors, Duhigg opines that: *"Our weak-tie acquaintances are often as influential—if not more—than our close-tie friends"*.

Such an idea chimes well with all those who stress the oddly intense authority that perfect strangers can wield over our lives and the decisions which drive them forward. Every day, our fellow shoppers on **eBay** and **Amazon,** with whom we may well never communicate directly, freely signal good deals to us and nudge us away from bad ones. These days, big hotels are so reconciled to the global super-power that is **TripAdvisor** that if one guest complains post-visit about a microscopic stain on a shower curtain then the Hotel Manager will promptly report, immediately under the same post, that the Head of Housekeeping has been put on a charge.

Brands fear, oh how they fear, the voice than can reach the back of the network. And in cyberspace, almost every consumer can be an opera singer. If you have ever thought about buying a digital camera, then when you go online you will find a running commentary on the products available and all their uses and features and performances—a commentary from all sorts, from the teenage geek-expert to the Dad in San Francisco who was just a little disappointed with the responsiveness of a certain brand's high-speed auto-focus function at his daughter's birthday party and wants to give you the tip-off. What a brave new world, as Shakespeare would say today, that has such generous consumers in it.

All this is, in a serious but ultimately limited way, proof of consumer rationality at work. Busy people, about to buy, see a red light starting to flash. It does not matter who is holding the torch. No sale. There are those in the business consultancy world who have openly questioned whether it is correct any more to see consumers as distinct, self-standing entities at all; for them, the reality of the individual consciousness is not in fact a reality but rather a crude paraphrase of the true business of living. Learned studies record just how lemming can be the behavior of financial traders who buy a particular stock for no obvious reason other than the fact that the man across the floor in another green jacket seems to be buying rather a lot of it this morning. The construction boom in Ireland of the 00s decade is also often invoked; firms started acting as if the entire population of the country was *each* going to need a bungalow on the Wicklow coast and would be able, whatever his/her objective circumstances, to pay for it. The result was, of course, acres of empty, boarded-over and vandalized houses.

How would the finest social scientist of the Western world explain to our friendly academic visiting from a far distant galaxy and keen to learn the ways of earthlings just how Ponzi schemes succeed? The herd who followed Bernie Madoff were presumably motivated by, yes, the promise of financial returns greater than the market average; but did the fact that so many investors, including many celebrities, were on board massively expand the audience for the fraud? Darn tootin'. How could so many perfectly smart people, our friend from Andromeda might wonder, not stop to think for themselves instead of joining hands with strangers in an act of shared financial astigmatism, a **Big Lie** if ever there was one? And while we are on the subject, he might further question, exactly *why* is Paris Hilton so popular? Does *anyone* really like raw fish? What *is* it with Gangnam Style? And just what drives so many English men to believe that khaki shorts and open-toed sandals with grey knee-length socks make for appropriate Mediterranean beachwear? Seen from some angles, there may not be any genuinely independent people at all. One mad bird takes a lead and a million starlings swoop behind.

In our search for insight-heavy conclusions amid this story rich in paradox, there is another crucial aspect. Few consumer-citizens might like to admit that they are easily influenced to live any part of their lives according to the established preferences of others—though many plainly are. Meanwhile, many of them just love to wield influence over others and see that influence endorsed. (And they are the same people—the "non-influenced" and the "influencers"). It is a form of 21st century human satisfaction, both peculiar and profound, to know that you have posted a stinking review of the latest Matt Damon movie and that at least a few potential theater-goers will be discouraged. Or directed a family you will never meet to the best place to stay at **Disneyland**. Or shared your views about the best-smelling exfoliating body scrub on the market at less than $10 a pop. There is no market left, from toothpicks to trampolines, which does not have its very own commentariat. The reward for all this unsolicited activity has to be some kind of self-elevation, the sound of distant applause.

Of course, many a brand takes a ride on this phenomenon. Look at those which put a little spot commercial at the opening of a clip on **YouTube**, a website which celebrates this whole urge to show-and-tell. Some supermarkets now run networks of wine-lovers wherein fans of crisp Burgundy whites can direct other drinkers to this year's best Côte d'Or. In some of its outlets, a brand like **Diesel** allows one's **Facebook** friends to comment in real time on the suitability of an outfit one is thinking about buying. The **Diesel Cam** kiosk lets a customer upload images of herself in the new top and await the group response. As ever more sophisticated augmented reality machines become available in fitting-rooms across the globe, there will be no stopping fashion shoppers triggering a reaction from friends and strangers alike amid a viral catwalk and an in-built instant-response mechanism. Across many mature and maturing economies, there are already so many apps which deliver a version of this; **Fashion Assistant** and **Cloth** are cases in point within a fast-evolving market. There is, moreover, a fantastic initiative from DBB in the form of the **Stockholms Stadsmission *You'll Never Wear That Again,*** a platform on which people use social media to hold a running debate on the quality (or not) of their fashion choices, now and over the years.

Nobody need ever buy an ill-fitting business suit or, seduced by a *Suits-You!* in-store sales assistant, a yellow tie for a polka-dot shirt again. The call of the claque will see us all through. The same basic story will be ever more true, *mutatis mutandis,* as we browse for books, select toys for our kids, choose a present for a lovely but difficult-to-please spouse. In the sense we mean here, solitary purchasing will be reserved for cigarettes, hangover treatments and novels bought in out-of-the-way bookstores—those paperbacks which have an embossed image of a pair of handcuffs on the front. For the age we inhabit, social purchasing—the active and immediate presence of a group surrounding and influencing an individual moment of choice—will do nothing other than swell.

Looked at crowds from both sides now

It somehow seems more acceptable to take both *strong-tie* and *weak-tie* advice—tips from people we like and from people we do not know—in order to regulate our consumption and maximize its value. Alongside this, we are more uninhibited about, say, marrying or living with whom we want and, in the world of faith or politics or culture, believing and preferring what we want, more so than our grandparents were able or willing to do.

Consider the way, in this latter sense, in which the whole concept of *lifestage* is not the force it was. As you move out of your teens and into (now generally much later) family formation and then into middle age (with your kids still, rather unexpectedly, living at home) and forwards into what is hardly any longer called the third age . . . so you find that the social conventions which once accompanied each age bracket are not as powerful they used to be. In Future Foundation, we abbreviate this theme into the trend **Ageless Society**. It references the reality that, for instance, that there are ever fewer brands which exclusively address specific age groups. It is not hard to find examples of this story at work. Brands such as **Dolce & Gabbana**, **Marks & Spencer**, **American Apparel** . . . have in recent years all run famously age-inclusive promotional campaigns which offer a very direct welcome to the silver-haired customer (without, presumably, discouraging the young and the trendy).

But even within this essentially benign development, the social norm stings and that **Big Lie** sings. As a crude summary, let's propose that while few of our *past-the-first-flush-of-youth* co-citizens may say they need help to delay or distort the ageing process, the market for just about every conceivable product in this general anti-ageing category continues to expand. From our Future Foundation quantitative surveys, we can learn that only around 18% of Americans aged over

55 will agree that, were they wealthier than today, they would buy more and better toiletries and cosmetics; (a similar level of response is generated in other parts of the world). Less than 10% of Americans aged 45 to 54 strongly agree that they would consider non-invasive surgery (such as Botox, teeth whitening . . .). Hardly anyone in the same bracket agrees strongly in Western Europe.

And yet. **ASAPS**, the trade body for aesthetic surgeons in the US, reports that between 2001 and 2011 there was an 80% increase in the number of procedures done on people over 65. This includes everything from brow lifts to liposuction to the full range of skin revivifying techniques—and even rejuvenation procedures for parts of the body too delicate to discuss here. In fact, over a third of all surgical and non-surgical procedures in the US are now requested by citizens over 51. From 1997 to 2012, according to the same source, American men's participation in this market increased by 106%. One can hardly think of a country where the body sculpture sector is not doing well. The relevant UK trade body, **BAAPS**, reports that even as the UK economy was passing through the unpleasantness of double-dip downturn the anti-ageing procedure market was enjoying a double-digit growth. The collectivized obligation to look attractive at any age is so emphatic that many easily and readily submit. At the same time, we can safely assume that many who do so derive real personal satisfaction from smoother skin and thinner waists—and the consequent sense of continued membership of the bold and the beautiful for as many days of their lives as possible.

However, openly admitting to researchers that one has buckled to a social pressure here seems inappropriate. Just why admit that chemical help was needed or work was done? For many of the world's most beautiful female celebrities any open discussion about one's procedures is a mega no-no taboo. This phenomenon in itself intensifies the sense that the appetite for a breast enlargement or a chemical peel should *not be acknowledged by anyone.* Even though it will certainly be true to trend analysts who look into this story that people—mostly women—in emerging markets are more open and ready to talk about their requirement for appearance-support products, it is the case that it is a small minority (often less than 10% in Europe and the US) who will strongly endorse the idea that cosmetic products are essential to them. It is a very dynamic irony at work here: the pressure to improve looks and repudiate ageing *on a generally shared and socially reinforced model* is intense while personal inhibitions against openly acknowledging such pressure stay resilient. We do not see any of this changing.

The expert, the influencer—and the de-personalizing of clout?

Our story for now has to conclude with a reflection about the expert in our midst, the person who embodies or is thought to embody serious knowledge to a depth which a regular individual could not easily or quickly achieve on her own. Of course, the expert can be a brand or an institution, any force able to establish and protect social orthodoxies in the major theaters of life. The editors of **Vogue** magazine help dictate the contemporary definition of beauty and elegance. Each time a **Michelin** star is awarded, a certain understanding of what constitutes fine dining is re-affirmed. When Sheryl Sandberg launches her **Lean In** movement, on the back of her spectacular success as a woman in business, so her ideas about career-advancement become an entire solidarity for those women, perhaps juggling and struggling with traditional pressures and prejudices, all across the world.

We might ask what the future holds for such phenomena. Will expertise be packaged differently for us, presented in more *me*-shaped ways? This decade is already seeing the birth of what we can call hyper-relevant networks—brands, websites, blogs, apps . . . which can be ever more responsive to one's own portfolio of interests and needs. These can often deliver concentrated advice from like-minded souls about the quality of local gyms to crime control in a particular neighborhood. The core proposition of **Google Circles**, for instance, is: "Share and receive updates from the right people". Along the way, as we reference above, consumers seem generally more willing to acknowledge the impact of advice from family and friends. And, of course, there are to be more and more moments of decision at which we can activate our personal histories, ie when we have personalized data management systems that can recall what we once bought, whom we sought for guidance when we bought it, whether or not there was a satisfactory performance from the product or the service.

So, must group norms weaken over time? Will more trust be pro-actively placed in highly individualized sources? Is the universal expert's day done? And will we all be content that our choices have become super-focused, algorithmically perfected, liberated from any tendency to follow the empty herd?

"I generally dislike shopping and do not really do any research when it comes to saving money, nor do I check out catalogues, in the supermarket I generally have a photographic memory and instantly know which products are of value and which products are the more expensive brands and are overpriced. This has evolved over years of product trial and error and includes homebrand products".

Female, 45-54, mother, New South Wales, Australia

Let's try to answer.

It must be a possibility that there is something changing, something evanescent within all this frictional interaction between the group and the individual in its commercially relevant manifestations. Perhaps ultra-smart systems will so filter and activate only the best advice from the best of sources that consumers—in numbers serious enough to matter—genuinely cease consuming on the basis of whimsy and habit and ignorance. Perhaps inefficiency is indeed about to be deported from millions of lives and millions of decisions, right up to the point where we totally optimize our choice of new car or birthday gift or dietary supplements or winter vacation resort. Just as one day soon, I will drive along Interstate 280 without actually doing any driving myself (courtesy of fabulous car caravanning technologies) so I will have pre-programmed so much of my wider decision-taking to do without my individual discretion, ie good choices (tapping all the best wisdoms) will be provided and actualized for me.

So, in such brave new worlds, brands face an Olympian task to bring direct, unfiltered, one-to-one, "buy me" messages to customers or to motivate crowds of those customers' fellows to spread the good news in socially discursive ways—to the effect that this is a funky bar and that this fragrance is really dreamy and that this watch will make you, at least in the wrist department, resemble a movie star.

We touch here the great marketing issue of the age. Not much room for the Three Ps here. All we will say for now is that perhaps the **Big Lie** story, as elaborated in all the foregoing and still-to-come, represents some good news for insight.

For perhaps, as the years pass and systems grow more super-efficient, it will still be true in ever evolving ways that nobody likes to admit that she is easily influenced. There will be, let us dare to predict, rebellions against too much programatic, pre-processed choice-making. Smart brands will, the other point of the pincer, find new ways to build a dialogue with consumers which implicitly acknowledges that we all like to act as if we are indeed in charge and not a pipe to the advertiser's finger to sound whatever stop.

It is unlikely that the buzz millions seem to get from giving free advice to others (and seeing that advice converted into action) will dwindle away from the social square. After all, consumption is meant to lead to performance-satisfaction. What if your lovely but difficult-to-please spouse tells you she dislikes the car you have just, after taking advice both frivolous and studied, brought into the driveway? What if your young man, plainly disliking his linguine, asks you why you picked this restaurant for his birthday treat? What if you hated the ultra eco-friendly Mexican beach resort so heavily recommended by both neighbors and strangers online—on the grounds that you thought it was a complete rip-off—but do not want to sound un-green in any conversation about it?

Plenty of space left, even as inefficiency putatively ends, for error, cussedness, caprice, disappointment, laziness—and lies, big and small, of all sorts.

Intuitions for Insight

- The electricity that passes from group to individual and back again remains the most dynamic form of energy for commercial insight and strategy to measure and harness.
- Any analysis of the social pressures on individuals to conform to certain attitudes and behaviors should be built on the assumption that more changes in life than stays the same. The best branding does not rest on what was presumed about all aspects of consumer culture—including earlier versions of the **Big Lie**—even a decade ago.
- It is, however, a singularly resilient example of the **Big Lie** that, even in a so much better educated and so much smarter century, hardly a living soul will admit to being influenced by the marketer's craft. It remains a social curiosity that many want to exercise influence over others just as most do not themselves want to be considered the easily over-influenced kind.

- If anything, systems which deliver the very best of consolidated advice (when buying a car, choosing a vacation, selecting a cocktail dress . . .) will give rise to new versions of, variations on, the **Big Lie** proposition. No-one should assume the death of suck-it-and-see economics or of heuristic behavior in general. Coats worn one day by a young duchess in England or a winter songstress on a red carpet will still mysteriously disappear from shelves. In any market with a fashion dimension, shoppers will still want to know what is smart for today, in every sense of the word—and will not always be able to work it out for themselves.
- Much has been made about the tactical requirement to locate and motivate special influencers, early adopters, mavens . . . But in the age of the consumer review, it is noticeable how many ordinary individuals can be influencers across so many markets, if they so choose.
- The more people like to claim influence, the less they are probably wielding. The **Big Lie** can effect consumers in all their different modes—*influenced* and *influencing*. Could it be that early adopters might claim influence, when in fact their signals do no more than predict or corroborate what is going to happen anyway? An early online review in favor of a new movie or book might merely foresee a product that was going to be widely purchased and enjoyed in any case.

CHAPTER THREE

COMFORTABLE LIVES,
UNCOMFORTABLE TRUTHS

Questions for Analysis

- All market research findings require careful mining. By what principles should brand leaders understand their limits while drawing maximum value from them in pursuit of ever better protected market positions?
- It is a good working notion that the more delicate the subject matter the more inhibitions to complete truthfulness will define consumer responses. How should we apply this notion in the field of eco-sensitive opinion and its possible relationship to eco-sensitive buying behavior?

- To what extent does the general awareness of environmental anxieties and ethical dilemmas in general shape what consumer-citizens think they ought to do and to say in life, from day to day?
- How do those consumer-citizens think they reconcile the demand for restraint and the urge for pleasure? And how might the insight trades creatively intervene to understand and perhaps solve/salve any such practical contradictions?
- If celebrity today is a kind of consumerist sainthood, then how should we understand the attempts of civilian-consumers to mimic the lifestyles of the rich and famous? Will the itch to upgrade always trump the appeal of restraint?

The failure of polite enquiry amid the need for knowledge

To *our* knowledge, there is among us no super-wealthy philanthropist who would like to devote massive funds to the cause of just knowing what people think. There is, perhaps regrettably, no opinion research equivalent of **Hunger Games**, where only the remorselessly well-informed survives. To our further knowledge, no research company is anywhere under the direct control of the Corleone family and its unique way of doing business.

But what fun it would be if researchers could be somehow licensed to do *anything they had to do* in order to pull the cold truth out of consumers' hearts.

There could be soft and hard applications of such an idea. Let's imagine that an extremely adventurous and preposterously well-resourced quantitative agency decided to pay a national sample of consumers some $10,000 each to participate in a simple survey. And the content of the survey touches such issues as a) corporate ethics in the modern world b) the role of personal anxieties about global warming within lifestyle choices and c) sources of dominant authority in our lives. (We pick our suggestions pointedly here). Would the results be materially different from those generated if respondents were, equally innovatively, each *charged* $10 to participate?

It's a thought. Let's walk further.

Would that promise of a substantial financial reward put people under psychological pressure to reveal *more* about what they truly think? Or make no difference? Or would it induce respondents more readily to assert anything that they thought the research company—for a few moments, in a sense, their employer—*wanted them to say*?

What impact—an interesting bifurcation—would it make if those paid the $10,000 were to have their names published in, for example, **The Huffington Post**, alongside a summary of their most salient opinions, for all their friends and co-workers to read?

We can hardly imagine that under the wild swing of such variations the set of answers to specific questions would remain constant. This is the very electricity of the **Big Lie**.

We can think about this insinuation another way round. What if big men with names like Jimmy the Swordfish or Tito "Scar Tissue" Pieroni were beckoned to leave their current careers in debt collection on the East Coast and join the qualitative research industry? Would their specialist persuasion skills produce the very chunkiest gobbets of truth, unseasoned by social expectation, undiluted by any workaday distortion?

We can see the scene in the focus group. Tito, the clever one, speaks:

*Now listen good, Mrs. Aronowitz. I'm going to ask you one more time. And if you do not tell me now **exactly** how much—look again at the 1 to 10 scale on the table here—you really care about public* *investment in renewable energy then Tilly your lovely Labrador will not see another dinner time. You know what I'm saying?*

The serious point we try to make is that interrogations of consumers are, out there in insight-needy land, generally formal, polite, well-manicured affairs. Nobody can be bribed and nobody can be threatened. Even gentle cajoling is not allowed. No $100,000-an-hour cross-examining attorneys. No *Frost-Nixon* here.

Of course (we hear what you are thinking), there are many industry-recognized techniques for trying to probe surface opinion in order to weigh the views that might lie beneath (while other views lie, so to speak, up front). But the fact persists that no professional body in the field of market research either recommends or permits the use of the polygraph. (We are not aware of too many polling studies from the 1950s. But had the question ever been asked: *Do you subscribe to **Playboy** magazine?*—then we suspect that the affirmative replies might well have been, on a national male sample, close to zero).

More, some in the intellectual wing of the research trades may be found talking a lot about such phenomena as *social desirability bias* and *fundamental attribution error* as if they were marvellously explanatory ideas or even techniques. They have to recognize though that they are hardly bringing debate to some kind of orderly conclusion by invoking such references. To argue that consumers might well want to present a good image of themselves in any conversation about their lives or that they may not always be aware of exactly why they went to a particular store and bought a particular pair of shoes on a particular day is—surely—to write the first paragraph of insight, not the closing, clinching chapter. It's all that brands and institutions should be prompted to *do* about such features—the specific ways in which they might *profit* from them—that counts.

At this point, we offer this axiom. The spirits who govern our individual thoughts about *how we all ought to behave in life* and *how we should define our responsibilities* towards local/regional/national/global co-citizens . . . are born and reside in the darkest caves of all. They will emerge fully into the light but rarely. And they will speak, when invited, in many tongues.

As we say elsewhere, *all* human answers to research questions are valuable and add to insight—whether they represent the settled will of the respondent or not. But for the theme under debate in this chapter, the interpretive equivalent of a jackhammer will be required to break through into some light.

Do consumers dream of green sheep?

We might well want to argue that the **Kyoto Summit** of 1997—and all the internationally shared agreements and commitments to which it gave rise—represents not so much the birth of modern environmentalism within public policy as the end of its adolescence. From then, it becomes a universalism that the production of greenhouse gases has to be firmly regulated in the common good for those living today and those who will live through multiple decades to come. Though the pulse of Kyoto was significantly weaker in the US (which refused, unlike the EU, to become party to the Kyoto Protocol), anxiety about global warming became a drumbeat here too. In 2006, the publication of Al Gore's **An Inconvenient Truth** and the subsequent movie-documentary drove the story big time and downtown.

The long zig-zaggy path of the politics of global greenery **(Rio+10, Copenhagen Summit**, **Rio Earth Summit** . . .) need not detain us here. For we can simply juxtapose such energy as has been put behind all such attempts to address planetary warming with a pretty well worldwide acceptance on the part of citizens. Most of them will agree that a) the threat implied to human wellbeing is real enough and b) something could and should be done about it. In polite society in many parts of the world, to deny the power of unchecked greenhouse gases to rot the planet is to risk being painted—perhaps even shunned—as morally feeble, easily duped, stupidly contrarian or worse.

Across this century, eco-sensitivity has become a principal expression of moral motive inside the evolution of modern consumerism.

This said, let's put down a vital piece of empirical foundation here.

In his speech accepting the **Nobel Peace Prize** in 2007, Al Gore told his global audience:

"We, the human species, are confronting a planetary emergency—a threat to the survival of our civilization that is gathering ominous and destructive potential even as we gather here. But there is hopeful news as well: we have the ability to solve this crisis and avoid the worst—though not all—of its consequences, if we act boldly, decisively and quickly".

In April 2012, Connie Hedegaard, the first ever European Commissioner for Climate Action and a Member of the **UN Secretary General's High Level Panel on Global Sustainability**, declared at the **Cop18** event in Doha.

"Ladies and Gentlemen, we don't need more torrential floods, more storms and devastating droughts to tell us that time is running out.

Honestly: We do not have to wait for more reports to do the right thing. What we need now is progress. Progress on our common journey to a world with a stable climate and equitable access to sustainable development.

Our people expect it.

Our economies need it.

Our planet craves it.

Remember: we can bail out banks. We can bail out states. But no one can bail out the climate, if we don't get our act together".

In a famous moment at an event in Ohio during his Presidential campaign, Mitt Romney found himself provocatively asked by a voter: *Do you still think the rising of the seas is funny?* Now, Governor Romney had his answer to this and had indeed previously written down his views about the reality of climate change. But the bitter, almost sarcastic tone in the question is, for us, the point of our point.

Those voices who demand action to stop environmental despoliation speak often in a quasi-biblical *apocalyptese*. We, the authors of this book, are not here with you in this moment to say that they are wrong to do this; nobody says that the planet is not at grave risk from one cause or another. But what animates our thinking is the effect that this intensity of debate and this strength of language have on all the people living in Georgia, Gansu, Galway . . . When important, well-meaning, high-ranking public figures tell you that the eco-system is under immediate attack; when this proposition resonates through your media via vocal and passionate lobby organisations; when your 5th Grade daughter comes home from school to show you her color drawing of the sadly disappearing Iberian Lynx . . . the invitation to walk more than a mile in the ecologist's shoes is, socially and emotionally, irresistible.

Such is the hubbub of general anxiety about climate change and the life-devouring disasters to which it could give rise that it becomes extremely hard for the insight professional to know what people privately believe and, more crucially, on which beliefs they will actually act.

In fact, for our **Big Lie** proposition, modern eco-ethics come to us as something of a perfect storm. As follows:-

- Relatively few politicians will, whatever priority they would privately prefer to give to green agendas *had they untrammelled discretion*, wantonly incur the anger of powerful eco lobbies or confound by now deeply embedded public assumptions about the threats to the planet

- Relatively few individuals (whatever they might think of the *causes* of global warming—a big dispute in the US) will feel comfortable about saying out loud that, *what-ev-er*, they just do not care about the planet and feel no personal responsibility at all for preserving its wellbeing
- Many companies operating in specially eco-sensitive sectors (energy, construction, food & drink, mobility and travel, clothes and fashions . . .) are left with the problem of trying to clarify what their customers truly think and really want.

Given what they say to our opinion researchers about their eco feelings, do our customers genuinely crave more green products?

*Are they really willing to pay more for ever **greener** products?*

Will they switch to competitor brands if we do not continuously scale upwards our green credentials?

Do they just want to hear us sounding ecologically sensitive but are never actually going to track or even value the detailed things we do in this field (water economy, waste management, reduced packaging . . .)?

What is that we really know and what should we really do?

> "Younger healthy people are more worried about global warming and are more vigilant about corporation environmental impact. I researched for smart phones which would use less natural resources and have better labor standards when switching my phone last time, but could not find one better than the other, so it ended up not being a factor".
>
> **Female, 29, NYC, USA**

We add a trend analyst's observation at this point. Probably like other agencies, Future Foundation has noticed that consumer answers to questions about green issues may well vary according the interview mode. Specifically, a question which addresses the theme of *how-much-do-you-personally-care-about-the-planet's-problems* has so far tended to generate more positive *yes-I-do-care* answers if the question is asked face-to-face than if the question is answered in an online survey.

This many not sound all that surprising to some. But the example does bring home again the transcendent importance of what we will call *detachment within inquisition*. Moreover, our general assumption would be that any such difference between f2f and online will stay no more stable over time than any difference between, say, answers given on a smartphone app while commuting to work and answers given while sitting at home on a relaxing Saturday afternoon. Behavioral conventions, social norms, established habits, levels of comfort with technological innovation . . . naturally shift, not always very fast but frequently enough. Insight professionals know that opinions bend as time dilates, as what were once the attitudes only of early adopters today turn into social conformities.

We all must (say we) care about the eco-system.

If Einstein had built his career in an advertising agency he would have applied the theory of curved space to consumer-brand communication. Simple gravity—*Do you think we should all recycle more? Yes I strongly agree!*—just will not suffice.

Eco-etiquette and the deflation of excess

There is no doubt that the ethics of modern environmentalism can give the consumer a lot of work to do. Indeed such ethics might be thought to contest the very status or *rank* of consumer, the very motives behind the purchase of all lifestyle furniture above and beyond the satisfaction of basic human needs. The consumer has to process some inner arbitration between appetite and restraint, discipline and indulgence.

Of course, there will be citizens going to the shops this afternoon who will never ever give an organic **Fairtrade** fig for the extent of desertification in littoral Africa or even the scale of recent Mid-West droughts. But many might well feel at some point in the consuming day at least a little eco-conflicted as they consider which detergent to buy, which new car to choose, whether to make that three mile trip to the local recycling facility, whether to book a long-haul vacation, whether to burn logs in the stove, how many plastic bags to use at the supermarket . . . Eco-sensitivity sets up interference patterns around so many everyday choices.

"A sense of pride is associated in how many green products are in your shopping cart. However, this is seen in upper middle class (and higher) families. People on a budget, including myself, have to make tougher decisions on green products; saving the environment is only a small factor in my purchasing power, the product still has to work and be economical. Yet, if there was a green cleaner for the same price as a caustic, not eco-friendly cleaner, I would research the product for reviews on cleaning power and if it is capable of the intended purpose I would purchase it".

Male, 28, married, Houston, TX, USA

One of the most telling impacts of 21st century eco-sensitivity is that it depresses the role of flamboyance in consumer culture, certainly in the West. Display—of personal success, of newly procured luxury goods—has to be discreet. It is just not cool and certainly very un-green to swagger. Nobody vrooms down Geary Boulevard in an open-topped **GranCabrio MC** smoking a **Cohiba Sublimes** with the **iPod Classic** playing *Crazy, Crazy Nights* by **Kiss** so that the whole city can hear. Naturally, the economic misfortunes that befell much of the Western World after 2008 invite society at large, even the wealthy in its midst, not to tempt fate. (To those who might think about acting in such a way, two words can be waggled: **Lehman Brothers**).

It is also just plain bad karma to mock with hip-opulence those struggling to prosper on low incomes or fighting to hold fragile jobs. Greed has not been officially good for a long time now. But also under the flag of today's environmentalism, however and wherever defined, excess is always abhorred and indulgence always questionable. In such a setting, consumption itself can seem insensitive. Besides, there are just so many day-to-day questions to be resolved. *Should my kids eat genetically engineered salmon? Or canned tuna? Should my car be hybrid? Should our home have LED lightbulbs?* With so much pressure-group campaigning these days and so many definitions of the eco-optimized life competing for social and political favor, the self-interrogation over how to live well can so easily be a something of a maze. *And, as I try to resolve all this, how much of that living well do I need to put on display? In how much, as it were, **eco**-flamboyance should I indulge? How much disapproval might I stimulate from my social peers if I display nothing or little?*

Meanwhile, one of the analytical beauties of globalization is that it presents so many different—let's call them—laboratories of consumerism.

In China, for instance, a pulsatingly expansionary middle class is showing a voracious appetite for the good life, for simple but plentiful treats all the way up to 24 carat luxury. Marketing Directors in such sectors as scotch whisky, overcoats, watches, shoes, sports cars, claret . . . must watch this consumerist klondike with a mix of both grateful reverence and slavering excitability. Meanwhile (and how interestingly for our thesis here), the political leadership of the PRC has openly deplored what they identify as a socially destabilizing and morally suspect culture of consumerist excess—a mood which has notoriously resulted in the interdiction of certain forms of visual advertising for luxury goods. Against this picture, Future Foundation has for some time been asking a sample of Chinese middle class people some conventional questions about their lives and times. Here are some outcomes. Around 90% of our sample agree that: *Climate change is definitely happening.* A similar percentage agree that: *Companies which fail to care for the environment should be penalized.* A not too dissimilar percentage (ca 80%) agree that they are motivated by what they can personally do: *to help protect the environment.*

Now, one of the things that any analyst working in the field of international quantitative research will surely have noticed by now is that middle class respondents from BRIC can, when asked a question about anything, be very enthusiastic about anything. Survey questions, asked within this geographic precinct, across a very wide range of subjects do tend to generate a high level of agreement and what the **Spice Girls** used to call "positivity". Smart trends consultancies will try to control for this and will present data and offer interpretations accordingly. (Others will just show you the charts and let you figure out the meaning on your own). For now, let's speculate about the human reality at work.

Might we get to appreciate that:

a) Chinese consumers are accustomed to expressing conformist views in public about issues of the day—as an inevitable psychological consequence, so one might think, of life in a one-party state?

b) for those consumers, any sense that the very eco-sensitivities which they are so ready to affirm might or should represent some kind of block on the enjoyment of lifestyle-enriching goods has not yet registered? Or does not yet want to be confronted?

Once again, let's suggest—with the general proposition of the **Big Lie** in view—that no brand actively engaged in the recruitment of Chinese consumers today will sensibly ignore the scale of eco-concern as reported above. But no such brand should take too linear, too *surface* a view either. For as it sets out to grow long-term intimacies with often still, in a sense, fledgling consumers, it cannot say out loud and it can barely say in private: *We just do not believe that you are **that** green.* In brand-building, as in love, any relationship that hopes to last supports only so much candor in order to survive and prosper.

> "I am passionate about my core beliefs, and I don't mean religion, I mean fairness, equality, anti-ignorance. I'm not one for making a big hoo-ha about things but will usually point out when someone is in the wrong. I don't think it is essential to know all the ins and outs, i.e. I have no idea of the wording of the Human Rights Act or am I up to date with all current issues etc. I think if my mind and heart are in the right place that is more important".
>
> **Female, 35-44, UK**

In the EU laboratory, the last few years have come cursed with severe interruptions to the once stable flow of macro-economic growth. This has precipitated much re-writing of once smooth-flowing social trends. Public attitudes to environmental problems need special consideration in this very context. When people give answers to interviewers' questions what signals are they really emitting?

Whom to trust, whom to blame . . . and what to buy

We interrupt this bulletin, at this very point, to offer a brief comment on the theme of trust (discussed in this book *passim*). Much market research money—we are not sure we would naturally always use the word *investment* here—is devoted to probing opinions about big companies and their ethical standing in the world. An oft prevailing assumption (on the part of interviewers and respondents alike?) is that such companies are a) powerful b) can themselves freely choose to live a virtuous or a sinful life and c) may or may not be trusted to do good by their customers, their staff, the communities in which they do business. The results invariably reveal a low level of popular respect for corporate life and there are plenty of consultancies who will wave such findings—as they relate to specific business sectors and specific brands—in front of their clients, seeing the expressed lack of trust as a threat to marketplace success and insisting that business strategy should be adjusted accordingly.

But, if you think about it, asking people at large if they trust big companies is like asking soccer fans in Barcelona just how fond they are of **Real Madrid**. Or the audience at the **Grand Ole Opry** if they would care to hear a medley of the songs of Ol Dirty Bastard.

If anyone is asked to confirm a popular wisdom—no matter how shallow or how untutored that wisdom may in fact be—that anyone will probably do so. There are freely available surveys which reveal—not really the right word—that substantial majorities of Europeans feel that big companies do not care about the environment. This will be invoked as proof that companies must indeed improve their eco-performance, communicate better, parade their good works more efficiently, etc, etc, etc. But in plenty of cultures it will seem nothing short of naive for anyone to say that you should trust big business *on any subject*. Cynicism over the true motives of companies has long since become a thickly calcified collective predisposition. And so, there is a limit to the strategic legibility of answers to opinion research questions of this kind *if* (the trend analyst's real job) *no deeper interpretation is superimposed*.

> "I strongly believe that companies should be more transparent and allow their consumers and shareholders to experience their culture and their way of doing business".
>
> **Male, 52, social networker, NCAA sports fan, Bentonville, Arkansas, USA**

Moreover, let's confront the possibility that the Western world is home to millions of *citizens* who will agree that big business cannot be trusted to help preserve the eco-system and millions of *consumers* who have never been practically influenced by this opinion in their daily lives. Never boycotted an oil company because of a careless spill which threatened marine life. Never compared and contrasted the environmentally-friendly investment record of the banks where they might keep their checking accounts. Never been motivated to switch to those fashion houses which offer organic cotton and cruelty-free silk.

Of course, over the years, the actions and behaviors of some large companies must have demoralized consumer-citizens and led to persistent suspicions that any enterprise which is big and famous and has glossy offices is, generally, up to no good. The scandal that once was **Enron**, accompanied by so many other famous collapses in corporate virtue in subsequent years, makes sceptics out of entire consumer segments. And there will be some people who are genuinely and profoundly outraged by what they see as the gross, commercialized over-exploitation of the planet's resources, while living their lives and taking their marketplace decisions in devoted accordance with that view. And yes, there will be shoppers who think that **Levi's** decision to use exotically recycled materials in its **Waste<Less** jeans range is really groovy. Or who think that a service like **ecoATM** which pays cash for old cell phones and keeps them from landfill is a great idea. Or who will admire **Amazon's** decision to launch a site like **Vine** which sells green goods only—and indeed visit the site and buy stuff. But environmentalism has never/not yet become a mass consumer activism and opinion surveys in this field have to be interpreted, with appropriate tactical detachment, in this light.

We close our sub-story here with a national example. In 2012, nearly 80% of our French consumer sample told Future Foundation researchers that they agreed that: *Companies should concentrate on giving value-for-money and good service to their customers—and minimize their social responsibility activities.* This is not far from the same percentage who *dis*agree that: *There is no point in being environmentally friendly because personal actions make no difference.* Meanwhile, around 30% of our French respondents—a rather high figure in a troubled economy—have told us that they would be willing to pay as much as 10% *more cash* for grocery items if they could be sure that such items were ultra environmentally friendly. Do all of these three sets of answers represent a pure, unvarnished representation of French opinion? Is a pressure to conform at work in each one them? No. And. Yes.

Moreover, it is a truism and a confusion in this whole analysis that economic downturn imparts a special energy to environmentalist propositions. Reducing household energy consumption is a pretty natural thing to consider in a society where median incomes have doggedly refused to rise over recent decades.

Let's take a moment here. The facts are critical.

As US Census figures dramatically show, if annual median household income is now just over $60,000 then that figure is comparable *in real terms* to what was being earned by the average family *at the time of the First Gulf War.* Much has been written about the US's apparently structural inability to defibrillate the average income of Mr and Mrs Joe Soap. The point to stress is that growth in such incomes has been enfeebled not just by recession and the predictable vicissitudes of the trade cycle but by something deeper, something very hard for either public policy or private enterprise to identify and successfully address. This is a mystery more Highsmith and Coben than Greenspan and Krugman. Inevitably, to any trends detective offering insights and forecasts about consumer attitudes and behaviors in the US, this mystery of the middle-classes' missing money is the most reverberative theme of all. So important in fact that all trend analysis—in spheres technological, cultural, commercial—has to have a special American cut as a result. Whatever their current difficulties, for instance, Americans' European cousins have had, in this framework of personal finance, a very different experience over the last generation. It goes without saying that our **Big Lie** story is, in so many of its practical expressions, much influenced by such realities.

To continue. Driving less and thus polluting less also seems like a good idea when the worldwide price of a barrel of crude remains stubbornly over $100. And consumers, in conversation, will show that they understand the essentially benevolent nature of the eco-econ overlap here. As a Future Foundation trendspotter in Georgia told us in 2012, *"Five years ago, there were large sports utility vehicles in everyone's driveway. But now that it has become popular to be eco-conscious, hybrids are replacing those SUVs. It is also more wallet-friendly to be eco-conscious. So with the economic downturn there has been more of a push to save money and go green"*.

Now, a majority of US citizens even in the highest income range tell Future Foundation in our surveys that they carefully budget their finances each month. The explosion in online price comparison activity speaks, from market to market, of just how devoted millions now are to the idea of converting household budgeting into something of a profession, one offering ever higher rungs of personal attainment. Obviously, such trends can easily obfuscate true consumer motives. And perhaps many consumers are not, at heart, unhappy about living in times when any effort to minimize consumption of, say, energy is socially lauded—times when money is tight, times when nobody will be specially keen to talk about just how tight it might really be. At the dinner parties of the middle classes, the school-teacher who is financially struggling is unlikely to draw the conversation away from the latest series of **Game of Thrones** or this season's performance by the **Golden State Warriors** and down into his trouble over making his personal ends meet.

Of course, we factor here too the fabulous product innovations of modern times, inventions and apps which allow us to track and measure our footprint, ecological and financial. We think too of those offers which facilitate the sharing and the renting of goods. It is striking how often the promotional language behind such products emphasizes the eco-rewards—less waste, more recycling, more practical sustainability—when very direct savings to consumer pocket-books are clearly being delivered too. Consider as an example, the mission statement of the **Share Some Sugar** brand (through which neighbors can borrow a chainsaw, a lawnmower, a GPS system . . .). The company believes:-

In being resourceful and making the most of what we have. And . . .

It is our responsibility to care for the environment.

That neighborhoods should feel like communities.

We still believe what we learned in kindergarten, that 'sharing means caring'.

Meanwhile, a very popular service like **Zipcar** ("Wheels When You Want Them") talks to its customers in a very special green accent:-

Zipcar members save more than $500 (vs. car ownership). What would you do with an extra $500 a month? Many Zipsters put it back into their communities by buying local and sustainable products.

(Quoted from the company website in March 2013).

This mixing and merging of themes ecological and economic is a perfect **Big Lie** cocktail.

We turn, at this point, to open a package of sometimes under-observed truths.

Still voices, decent lives?

Most people are nice. Most are well-meaning. Many do not have it easy—not by a long way—but few in our midst exult in total selfishness or studied indifference or mindless triviality. Millions raise their kids really well and would never withhold a favor from a troubled neighbor. Many too would recognize the force in Bill Clinton's remark that *a lot of life is just showing up and hanging on.*

But doing the right thing and living the good life must sometimes seem strangely incompatible objectives *in the specifics of the day-to-day.*

For a long time, politicians of the center-left in the UK—to take only one national example of the general point—used to be pleased to read that high proportions of British citizens were keen for the government of the day to take measures to address family poverty through more effective redistribution. Some 60% of our UK sample told Future Foundation in 2011: *British people today should be more angry about inequality in society.* According to UK data from the **European Social Survey** of (also) 2011, more than 60% of them agree in particular that: *The Government should take measures to reduce differences in income levels.* Around the same time as the ESS poll, **Eurobarometer** was confirming that some three quarters of the UK thought that poverty there had *definitely increased* in the last twelve months. Meanwhile, according to the **British Social Attitudes Survey** it is but a stubborn one third only who think that: *The Government should redistribute income from the better-off to those who are less well-off,* a rather more deflating outcome for, say, activists in the **British Labour Party**.

Now, of course, there is a perfectly valid and always lively debate to be had about the optimal level of state intervention in any market economy, intervention designed in principle to reduce poverty and generally increase what economists used to call the welfare function. And, yes, we know that relative poverty (one's current income and wealth in comparison to those of others) is not the same as absolute poverty or the inability to procure the basic goods of life. Finally, we know that it will be perfectly coherent for some citizens to want poverty to be reduced while genuinely believing that any increase in their own taxes will not assist with this goal.

But just like their counterparts in the US or Australia or France, British people tend to have UK-shaped impulses about things. Asking those people if they think there is too much poverty around and that the Government really ought to do something about it (and that things are probably getting worse all the time) . . . is like asking if they think kids should drink milk every day or whether it's likely to rain during this year's Summer vacation. Some things are just cultural loose change and fluidly distributed norms, white noise for the common soul.

The proportion of British people expressing trust in political parties has (we are grateful to **Eurobarometer** for the numbers) not reached beyond 20% at any time in the last decade. But two thirds of those eligible to vote, we pointedly observe *en passant,* regularly do so in General Elections. Voting is not compulsory in the UK but millions keep voting for the parties and politicians they do not officially rate. Not for the first time, the vehemence of an opinion is no guide to the incidence of consequent behavior. The truth is that expressing mistrust, disappointment, disaffection in all matters political is as British as drinking warm beer under the brooding indigo skies while watching and waiting for any one Summer to stay long and hot.

Now, many British people (to continue with them for a little longer) might well consider themselves to be both liberals and radicals, outraged by perceived injustice, always ready to throw a bone to the underdog. They will readily ventilate dissatisfaction with their elected representatives (their performance, their pay, their policies . . .); deplore the money-grabbing sharp practices of big business; expect grocery prices to rise while product portions are surreptitiously reduced; abominate the fat bonus checks paid to City of London bankers; agree that the old folks are getting a pretty bad deal in this country; give, once grossed, vast sums to charity telethons for those down-on-their-luck as run by the **BBC** . . .

No Englishman ever walks into his local pub in the rolling Chiltern Hills to declare to his drinking buddies: *Tell you what. Our Prime Minister is a real genius and a fantastic bloke. And, you know, many once severe social problems do seem to be being progressively eliminated as the decades pass*—while calling on them to join a rousing chorus of *The Sun Has Got His Hat On, Hip Hip Hip Hooray*!

Social analysts and corporate strategists alike have tracked the interesting places where this trend can take us in countries like the

UK and indeed across the Western world. We refer here to the theme of **Pop Radicalism**. This proposition suggests that, in ways enhanced and accelerated by the Digital Revolution, consumer-citizen protests can flare suddenly and dramatically and then, suddenly but silently, cool. And, what is more, this very fact can create the basis for specially framed communications between brands and customers.

Some may be thinking that, with this latter sentence, we are now headed to a rather grubby place. But stick with us, please.

Millions of us cannot or simply will not devote a preponderant amount of time/money to the great politico-ethical issues of the age, whether global warming, climate change, African wars, gender inequality, malnutrition and malaria, child starvation, mistreatment of Asian employees . . . But protest, if occasionally joined, can validate us as good-people in our own eyes, providing a platform of sporadic expression of our best motives, the chance for a short set of stand-up ethics—while not actually representing any significant alteration in our life-outlook.

The **Occupy** protestors who surrounded St. Paul's Cathedral in London and invaded Zuccotti Park in New York City or City Square in Melbourne might be seen as human lightning rods for a more widespread but essentially more shallow protest-pulse within society at large. So much of Occupy-style activism, we note, is very colorfully organized (beautifully designed banners, art-enriched websites, enviably hip T-shirts . . .) and almost always eye-catchingly newsworthy. It becomes what Guy Debord and others such might once have recognized as a "society of spectacle" round which audiences appear, applaud, part-participate, vicariously exist for a passing moment. For many, a little rebellion at work, perhaps on the streets, from time to time can be something of a theater of moralistic expression, ad hoc but not insincere. Not everyone's cup of tea all this, we know; but for many any outburst of complaint resonates with an inner strain of random anger, hair-trigger disappointment with the bossy (and quite possibly the useless) people in power today, vague hopes for better times. And sometimes it could be just their cussedness on parade, an urge to shout along with the crowd, throwing open their bag of nameless frustrations along the way.

This is a delicate matter to discuss. But smart insight knows both the limit and the value of public engagement with radical causes when that public takes such causes into the heart of its consumption decisions. Carrying no cynicism on their part, smart brands often recognize that expressions of personal complaint have their fashionability, indeed what we might call their easy virtue and easy *virality*. It is so convenient these days to leave a handprint of one's dissatisfaction somewhere—on **ShoutAbout** or **Pocket Protest** or **Change.Org** ("What Will You Change?"), signing and petitioning or adding to the **YouTube** viewing tally for a clip exposing some atrocity by an African warlord—all the while releasing one's need to affirm an ideal of some kind. It can be just so *cool* to complain. And these days it is very easy to be a bit of a renegade in ways totally transparent to others, friends and strangers alike.

Protest in the 21st century can, in fact, take very little effort on anyone's part.

Now, since we know that this book is being read by insight professionals who study both their markets and their societies very closely indeed, let's dare to say again: we know what you, our readers, are thinking. You are reflecting on the occasions when you have been aware that consumer disappointment with a brand's personality or performance has turned into serious commercial consequences. We all recall the experience of **Fruit of the Loom** and the student boycott over what were claimed to be poor working conditions in Honduras. Many will more recently recall the **Hyatt Hurts** campaign run by **Unite Here**. Those longer in the tooth will remember **Shell's** decision, abhorred by environmental lobbies, to dispose of the Brent Spar in the North Sea and the related damage to gas station sales in the eco-sensitive German market. No CEO in her right mind would ever want to see her food & drink portfolio be the subject of any consumer mobilization led by **Greenpeace**. It surely can be very bad for business.

"Of course we expect companies to act ethically—they're in the public domain and with so much attention drawn to those who don't, really companies, big or small, have no choice but to. I must say I'm not the kind of person to protest or boycott a company that acts 'unethically' out of principle but I still like to remain informed and I'm sure if something bothered me personally I'd consider doing so".

Female, 24, trainee retail manager, Midlands, UK

But, in the main, do consumers like to see the mighty fall or just wobble? And, as we think on an answer, is it possible for creative brands to accompany those consumers at least a little way on the march down Main Street, those who want to go on the march in the first place? One can think of many brands in the US which seem instinctively to know that many shoppers want to feel morally comfortable or wantonly cussèd or a mix of both impulses—but also want the practical expression of this to be de-caffeineated, controlled, incidental. Of course, too often in this kind of analysis those shoppers are envisaged as standing on a giant meter stick with "Agree Strongly" painted at one end and "Disagree Strongly" at the other; as questions are put to them (about big business, whom to blame for the state of the planet, whether we have good governance these days . . .) they are notionally invited to take a stand on one of five points on the scale.

But life and the human emotions which inhabit it do not work like this. Those emotions are so many inter-woven wraps of fabric cladding surrounding people's hearts and minds. Cause and effect cannot always be used in the same sentence. The defining motive at work in any moment of choice can get very muffled.

When we say "Have a nice day" what do we mean?

The nicest, most well-meaning individual in our midst—we all know him—can have a truly gruesome day at the office thanks to his spectacularly stupid and quite probably sociopathic boss. He can discover when he gets home (after a much delayed commute in a train with ruptured air-conditioning) that the **IRS** is not at all happy with his latest return, not happy at all. He then has to listen to his normally placid spouse kick rough about the "stupid, expensive car" he has just bought . . .

And he sits down alone in his study for a much needed, gently restorative **Pacífico** or two only for the email to ping with a request to participate in a 20 minute online survey on Business Ethics in America Today with special reference to a) supply chain management within developing countries and b) the uses and abuses of corporate philanthropy. Who knows how he will answer such questions on a night like tonight, after a day like today? Life, morality, choice, appreciation of the planet's frailty, distress at the plight of others, absorption in private stress, loving the system one day, hating it the next . . . it does not easily quantify itself into a shiny ball of usable intelligence for those of us bringing stuff to market, does it? Sort out the truth of your lives, dear consumer-customers, and bring us a new prime number while you are about it. Research, huh?

The thing is, weaving once more into our **Pop Radical** theme, that you cannot actually sell ethics or eco-sensitivity. A customer cannot walk into **Macy's** or log on to **Amazon** and ask for two kilos of socially valuable outcomes. *It always has to come along with a product.*

Of course, in the modern world and even in sludged-up economies, many offers will show some and indeed often considerable respect for those consumer feelings and worries that lie beyond the consumption of the actual product bought. All car manufacturers try to produce clean cars; many an oil company gives advice about how to save fuel and show commitment to sustainable energy use; there are multinationals donating often colossal sums to buttress life-enhancing economic development in Africa and beyond. But all such things do not disguise the unchanging and essentially transactional relationship between company and customer—transactional but complex. A mother of two kids living in Pinesdale, Montana who is buying ice cream this afternoon might well be motivated by a particular brand's commitment to equal rights for all and to the health insurance needs of its staff. But the price of a pint, the depth of a discount, the quality of the taste, the arrival of new and attractive flavors, the promise of a nutritional benefit . . . all form interactive elements in her inner dialogue about what and how much to buy. And what to keep buying. To isolate and weigh her exclusive appreciation of the ice cream supplier's stance on the big issues of our time *at any given moment* is hardly something that is going to succeed and prove valuable on the basis of direct questioning alone. If you think we make too much of an obvious point here, let's recall that many research companies try to persuade their corporate clients to continue with sometimes massive quantitative and qualitative spend and *act as if powerful strategy-enriching revelations are always thereby being made.* The **Big Lie**, in its strategically unprocessed form, can thus be brought into the city of Troy not by the sneaky Greeks but in a wooden horse supplied by business consultants paid, perversely, by King Priam himself.

This is what, in our view, makes a trend such as **Pop Radical** such a powerfully organizing perspective. It speaks of the intermittent and contingent nature of the consumer's ethical expression and the actual type of satisfaction the consumer might take from being out-and-proud in her quest for social improvements and ethically responsible marketplace behavior.

In conversation, that expression might well be instinctively exaggerated. But no sensitive brand communicator will ever say to a customer: *Let's get down on it, here. You don't really care that much about just how it comes to pass that you are able to buy a pair of designer jeans for $50? Or 2lbs of honey-coated banana slices for only $8? Or a flight from London to Paris for an outstanding $40? You are not really worried about the incomes of textile workers or Central*

American farm laborers or even the amount of pollution caused by even a short haul flight, are you?

The goal is rather to use social analysis and, crucially, trend identification to intuit just how much—let's call it—generalized humanitarianism customers want, want a lot, want occasionally. And sometimes they might well just need, as they show up and as they hang on, to *feel* that they are doing something good. How to react to all well-appointed social themes within business strategy is human calculus. Not two plus two = *they want more CSR programs* or *we need to be 15% more green.* Caring is just another form of currency, like money or time or attention; nobody wants to spend it all at once or give away more than they have.

> "I look for companies to act in an ethical and responsible way. If I find a company has not done this, I stop patronizing them. But I am enough of a realist to recognize that my definition of ethical and responsible is not the same as the definition used by others".
>
> **Female, 62, high school graduate, Baltimore, MD, USA**

How much non-discipline do disciplined consumers inwardly demand?

We turn now to complete our story of **Comfortable Lives, Uncomfortable Truths.** Our collective tolerance of life's random supply of work pressures, family tensions, stupid bosses, boring days at the office, this month's nearly maxed credit card . . . is fueled by so many of those things which, if taken to excess, will damage us all the more. (And probably, for that matter, damage the planet along the way too). We need treats, indulgences, tools of fantasy and reverie . . . plus those moments of just plain old letting rip. Without the tang of luxury in our lives or the distant hint thereof, would we all get out of bed in the morning still able to face the day?

At moments, sheer frivolity is also mandatory. Excess and exuberance sometimes too. Hardly a soul leads a perfectly monastic or puritanical existence. We do not need to spell out the frictions this can create inside the ethical and eco-sensitive self—and we discuss these presently. The whole engine of the market economy runs on the constant appetite for upgrade. How else to explain the appeal of a **Vertu** cell phone or some *grand cru* claret for your dinner party guests or a wedding gown spun from silk and platinum thread? Few markets have no deluxe dimension. We have gourmet TV dinners, designer pyjamas, boutique hotels, special edition malts, custom-made car shampoo, Japanese skin cream, wristwatches so elegant and wonderful they even tell you the time . . . A revolutionary improvement in the quality of the TV screen is doubtless being developed even as we write. **Jimmy Choo** is surely about to launch a new line of stunning pumps and wedges. A glossy brochure which has made you think about procuring your first-ever second home, close to some pretty exotic Winter sports resorts, popped into your mail box only this morning.

All this opens other discrepancies amongst all that consumer-citizens say out loud about their lives and what they privately think and what they, often/especially when nobody is looking, actually do. Inevitably, the **Big Lie** lurks.

How does the goal of a proper adult, take-my-responsibilities-seriously, well-lived life rub against the guzzling little demon that can pop up inside us? What *about* those who just wanna have fun and who do not necessarily want the truth but who do want something beautiful really rather a lot?

It is rare in much of popular culture for restraint to be lauded.

In modern times, let's reflect on just how funny/attractive can be the expressions of frothy youthful hedonism. We can think of everything from the **American Pie** movie franchise or the more recent **The Hangover** series or the **Road Trip** trilogy right up to **Spring Breakers**. There can hardly be a more *whether-you-like-*

it-or-not affirmative of excess-as-vitality. No song, meanwhile, ever became a Number One hit with the title **Let's Get Back To Math Class, Baby** or **I Cannot Come To The Party Tonight (Because Somebody Might Over-Indulge)** or **Best Not To Let It All Hang Out.**

In her book, **In Praise of Messy Lives**, Katie Roiphe reflects on the success of the series **Mad Men** on TV. She puts the appeal down to a conceptualizing narrative of "the thrill of casual vice" and "all that stylish chaos, all that selfish, retrograde abandon"—contradistinctive to all the middle class disciplines (the gyms, the organic food, the tobacco-free homes, the sheer "tameness of contemporary sins" . . .) which organize 21st century life for so many adults. In the light of such a proposition, one indeed wonders whether **Mad Men** is just a specially glorious version of many modern American escapologies, a super-subliminal indulgence fantasy, a nod and a pretty unambiguous wink to all those who inwardly bristle and bridle (and do more than that often enough) against the convention of sobriety. The TV series **Spartacus** did not portray Capua as a venue for hard-working families just trying to keep it real in dangerous political times but rather as a platform for the lubricious and the ruthless (whose occasional successes we are hardly ever invited to deplore). The protagonists of **Nip/Tuck** never said to new customers: *Yes, we can see why you like yourself so much.* **Sex And The City** was occasionally about restraints but so *never* about restraint. Look back on **Cashmere Mafia, Lipstick Jungle, Dirt, Swingtown, Boardwalk Empire** . . . This is a universe in which suppliers of cultural artefacts know that millions want the edginess of lifestyle risk to be the core of the story.

We check ourselves at this point to remember that we are still talking about the *same* consumer-citizens whose approach to the challenges of ethical consumerism and eco-sensitivity we were reviewing only a few moments ago. Situationally speaking, nobody—even the greenest in our company—can stay über eco-focused or on full scale *ethical consumption* alert all the time.

No twenty-something man goes a hot first date without mirror-checking the suitability of his **Armani** shirt or while in a state of advanced anxiety about the long-run energy generation potential of wind-farming. His date's hair will have been pre-beautified by a *because-you're-worth-it* volumizing shampoo, her shoes will be same-day new, her fragrance **Lady Caron**. The movie theater that they visit will be playing something light and fluffy with Matthew McConaughey or Katherine Heigl. Al Gore's latest book on the future of the planet will not be discussed over their late-night **Jose Cuervo** at the **Infusion Lounge**. Our hopes, our dreams, our pleasures ... must have their space, un-invaded by too much Socratic exchange. There are times when consumers just have a heat-seeking focus on what it is they, here and now and without further reflection and with little thought of restraint, actually want.

And yet, few consumers interviewed in opinion surveys seem to have the courage of their own whimsy.

Sleb Nation and the hunt for glamour

Consider the modern **Cult of Celebrity**. Why do people seem so reluctant to admit that they love following famous people, their lives and loves? If suppliers of showbiz gossip or fashion/lifestyle magazines or websites were to pay too much literal attention to what is said about such themes in surveys they would conclude that their market did not actually exist. Only around 40,000 people live in Monaco and yet stories about and photographs of Prince Albert and the wider Grimaldi family often fill the front pages of weekly titles all over Europe. The same holds good for the royal families of Spain, Denmark, UK, Netherlands ... as any quick glance at popular reading material on railway newsstands across the continent will confirm. Now, no European has ever sent a résumé to a prospective employer in which it is stated that *reading about the Royal Households of Europe, with special reference to the often scandalous love lives of young princes and princesses* is a major spare-time pursuit. And yet ...

When Future Foundation asks Americans about their feelings about celebrities, we find a similar reluctance. Only around 5% will strongly affirm that they do indeed enjoy finding out about their exploits. Though print titles have been having a rough time in recent years, **People** is still a circulation top-ten magazine in the US. Meanwhile, sites such as **TMZ, OMG, Perez Hilton** . . . attract millions of unique monthly visitors. So solid is the coverage that no movie star could ever so much as walk into a small town, mid-West coffee shop at 7am without being photographed, uploaded, blogged, tweeted—her companion scrutinized, her fashion critiqued.

> "People have always been fascinated with fame. I don't tend to engage with celebrity culture apart from reading features and interviews in magazines and newspapers. Aside from that it's not something I seek out. I see it as a form of entertainment and often inspiration if the person is famous for a talent.
>
> I am most interested in what they have to say, not where they ate last night or what they are wearing. I tend to be interested in the things that have some substance and that resonate with me".
>
> **Male, 33, London, UK**

And yet, hardly a soul will ever agree that he/she is influenced in what is bought for themselves or their homes by celebrity endorsement. But Taylor Swift fronting **Wonderstruck** is all around while Paris Hilton has her **Can Can**. Charlie Siem promotes **Eau de Nuit**. Natalie Portman wears **Tom Ford** to the Oscars. If the Duchess of Cambridge in the UK wears a dress from **Reiss** at a public engagement then the style sells out. Kim Kardashian and Brooke Burns drive sales of **Skechers**. Daniel Craig brings a heroic presence to the launch of the **Range Rover Sport**. This kind of promotional activity seems pretty banal when one starts making lists like this until perhaps one reflects further on, once again, the hidden hand of the **Big Lie**. When you ask questions of consumer-citizens, they will want to seem smart, sophisticated and often more than a little superior. They will not want to seem like the patsies of the Don Drapers of today. Few are going to say that their favorite book is the latest biography of J-Lo. Not that many men will say they select their jeans from the **William Rast** range because those jeans might make them look like Justin Timberlake. Our relationship with famous people is such that their influence over us and our choices is not to be recognized out loud—just like a secret love affair.

The vaunted promise of Behavioral Economics (reviewed *passim*)—which we know has attracted many insight professionals—can be interestingly introduced into this picture. The promise made to those professionals (across various versions of BE theory) is that if consumer-facing propositions are correctly/cleverly framed, then good, ie ever more rational, choices will be made by consumers (and/or socially valuable outcomes—less smoking, more eco-friendly behavior, better driving etiquette, whatever—will be secured by public authorities). Brands can use the precepts of BE to find competitive advantage, expand price premiums, protect profits. So the theory runs. And there are examples of good practice and commercial success within this story.

But really the cult of celebrity is, in so many of its commercial manifestations, something of a walking subversion of any such prospect. For using a movie actress to promote a skin care or rainwear or sunglasses range might well make no promise other than reflected sheen. In other words, there is really no *framing* possible just as there is no (or very limited) discussion about product price or quality. A famous person in a commercial is often there precisely to limit rational debate; for most of the time all that she/he provides is the impregnable heuristic of glamour. In its promotions, **Dior** never declares aloud: *Look, our famous models are more interesting/attractive/cooler than those fronting competitor brands*. Nobody is, in a way, invited to respond rationally to Charlize Theron. **J'Adore**, *nous adorons*. Simple as that.

Now, this is not to imply that every campaign using a Hollywood A Lister is bound to succeed or that such a presence will bring benefits to all brand-customer dialogue. But the cult of celebrity remains a well-lit psychological intersection of fantasy and admiration, a space where functional claims about products are pushed to the edge of perspective. As we survey 21st century consumers, the cult expresses a form of unconfessable avarice, an engine of continuously renewable cultural energy in favor of ever more elevated lifestyles. In a world where Lady Gaga has 35 million followers on **Twitter,** we can see that a force-field has obviously been erected against too much self-discipline, asceticism, all claims made in support of progressive de-consumerisation. From market to market, there is always froth-fun or a new premium experience waiting to be had. Few of us may want to accept or admit that we are thus so easily seduced. But *slebs* come promptly along remind us that such outcomes await and to help us off with our clothes.

For every invitation to restraint that the 21st century carries into our consumerist lifestyles there is another invitation waiting on the mantelpiece to buy ourselves a more carefree life.

> "Celebrity news is bombarded on us all the time, so I find myself reading because it's in my face all the time, which makes me feel I lose my time".
>
> **Female, 29, NYC, USA**

For many of us, the **Big Lie** is a vital way of dealing with the inescapable contradictions of the age.

Intuitions for Insight

- We are all consumers. Executives in marketing and advertising and sales departments live, in the main, on the same streets as their customers. Their kids go to the same schools. They vote in the same booths. They too tut and shake their heads as they watch the evening news. Few of them are motivated exclusively and savagely by either personal gain or the profit-expanding potential of the company for which they work. Everybody wants our future—economic, social, environmental—to be better than the past.
- This said, there is all the more value in the most finely nuanced appreciation of what it is that those customers, when asked, say out loud about their life and times. For they are not necessarily more ethically sensitive to life's wider problems and more demanding of change than those who help bring goods to market for them.
- The social pressure to conform to certain ideas can be a heartily good thing. Few will disagree that, whatever our constitutional freedoms to speak as we please, sexist or racist remarks appal and should draw a very critical reaction from those who hear them.
- But insight professionals have to work in the caverns beneath general principles and broadly shared norms. Hardly any person can so perfectly balance their consumption behavior so that she is never wasteful, never frivolous. Sectors such as soft drinks have—this very thought in place—long since sought to infuse their communications and NPD with sophisticatedly overlapping messages, referencing refreshment and responsibility in the same breath, as if they were talking to many personalities inside each customer's head.

- Many consumer markets will similarly continue to run on the creative tension between discipline and indulgence—with many customers indicating that, however defined, they would approve of more of the former while actually enjoying as much of the latter as they want.
- The overhanging question here is whether a return to robust and sustained macro-economic growth in the US and the EU will alter the tolerances in this story. Can we expect that consumer-citizens will be willing to embrace more issues (social, ecological . . .) and *say that they demand* more of companies when they feel more secure in their incomes and prospects? Will, in this sense, the **Big Lie** be magnified as it becomes even more socially conventional for individuals to accept and proclaim ever wider social agendas? We suggest that this is precisely how insight professionals should think about the future.

CHAPTER FOUR

THE CALL OF YESTERDAY, THE SCREAM OF THE NEW

Questions for Analysis

- The consumer-citizen's passion for the past seems to stand in contradiction with the apparently inexhaustible appetite for new, different and better things. What is the nature of the commercial opportunity this contradiction creates and *re*-creates?
- Why do nostalgic feelings come with such a sense of loss—seemingly more powerful than positive hopes for the future?

- There is always an expert to challenge any claim of human value emerging within the latest wave of technological or cultural innovation. Is this simply shallow nostalgia dressed in a graduation gown?
- Many brands try to associate themselves with happy feelings. When consumer-citizens are asked about happiness, by what decoding device should we interpret what they mean?
- Will the Digital Age ultimately render obsolete or moribund our collective affection for the past, superimposing a new communications language for companies and brands to exploit?

Nostalgia—everything it used to be . . . ?

The past, as someone once said, is a foreign country. They do things differently there.

Many of us think that they did things so much *better* there too. Is it not perfectly astonishing just how powerfully seductive—amid the **Digital Revolution** and the endless list of new wonders brought by the internet age—the lure of the past remains?

Everyone in any part of the communications business knows this all too keenly. There is hardly a successful politician in the Western world who has not at some point prospered by telling the audience that the nation can be great again; that the virtue we once had as a society can be retrieved and put back to work; that too much simplicity has gone from modern living and it's time to bring it home. Some version thereof.

Meanwhile, the marketing and advertising community knows that if a brand has any sort of history or heritage then, crudely, you can always do *something* with it.

Maybe your client's candy product cannot really compete on quality and price in today's marketplace. But the fact that the brand is soon to celebrate its 150th birthday will supply a useful differentiator when this back-story is creatively made known to the public. Nostalgia-messaging can—there are countless examples of this—be easily deployed as an emotional heuristic, a shortcut to feelings both warm and reassuring. For many a consumer, to hear invoked a brand's hinterland (when one genuinely exists) is to find a proxy for authenticity, as if durability alone buttresses that brand's functional value. Put your savings in our bank—*we have been around since the Revolutionary War.* It's OK to feed your kids our bread—*our first store opened in Boston in 1906.* Take your vacation in our island resort—*nothing much has changed here since the Conquistadors left.*

> "My loyalty to a brand is not always shaped by its quality, price or past experiences but by what its parent company stands for".
>
> **Male, 52, social networker, Bentonville, Arkansas, USA**

But we are rushing ahead and missing a primary question here. And the question is this. *Just why does this phenomenon exist?*

Take life. Never before in history have human beings had the chance of so much. The **US Census Bureau** will confirm that when President Nixon was at his first mid-term average life expectancy in the US was 70 years; at President Obama's second term it is nearly 80 years. **Eurostat** tells us that life expectancy in Spain, Portugal, Netherlands, Germany, Finland, Sweden, UK . . . has now broken the 80 barrier (but was broken by none as recently as 2000). According to the Japanese authorities, female life expectancy is now 86 years—even by 1980, it was ca 78. A generation ago, some members of the **OECD**—eg Estonia, Poland, Mexico, Turkey—were showing life-expectancy-at-birth figures which were in the 60s. They are all in the 70+ zone now.

We do not need to push out a heavy payload of proof here. Whether one looks at life expectancy, rates of child mortality, adult morbidity (and the measurable phenomenon of "compressed morbidity"—people living longer and healthier lives with fewer years of *ante mortem* sickness), access to healthcare and general wellbeing . . . one knows that millions of lives are a whole lot less precarious than they used to be. This can be known by anyone who takes the time just to skim freely available intelligence on all that happened to the world's wealthier societies as they raced through the closing decades of the 20th century and into the new.

Of course, it is not the same garden for everyone. There will be people in our midst who deprecate modernity for what, as they would see it, are very good personal reasons. Some, for instance, may regret the decline of religious worship within their country. Some may feel that life today is too complex, coldly and alienatingly technological—so many screens, machines, devices. And, of course, some of us, whatever the general improvement, will have run into the kind of bad luck that turns the past into a more roseate option all round. Even if unemployment falls to its lowest level since the days when the only job for any of us was keeping goats in the savannah, it is still 100% for anyone enduring it. Bad health, bereavement, loss of love, career failure, the abrupt arrival of poverty . . . can all make the claims of modernity quite insultingly shallow.

The past as power norm . . .

But none of this explains why the past stays so damn potent within our culture and our commerce.

Here is a quick anecdote from the UK. You do not need to be in the trends analysis trade to know that Christmas is like an annual World Series for brands and retailers there. It barely matters what you are selling: fragrances, chocolates, toys, books, shirts, pyjamas, carpets, movies, ornaments, vacations, electric toothbrushes, earrings, liqueurs, toasters, pens, shoes, flowers, magazine subscriptions . . . whatever.

But, as they say locally, it bloody well matters if your company fails to shift its yuletide inventory. At the first whiff of reindeer in the shopper's nostrils, your brand has to be good to go. A *great* Christmas leads to the Marketing Director being carried shoulder-high round Trafalgar Square by a delirious CEO. A *good* Christmas leads to a lot of executives clearing their desks, with yellowing mistletoe their only severance.

In 2006, Future Foundation for the first time asked British people to respond to the statement: *Christmas is not as much fun now as it was when I was growing up.*

We re-asked in 2009 and 2012. In each year of responses, an oddly stable 53% (let's call it a working majority) of *those under-24* agreed. In every other age group, there was, not surprisingly, a bigger majority still—*but not by that much.* Even those consumer-citizens who have limited life experience and who are still, by historical standards, quite a privileged generation feel that something has already been lost among the chestnuts roasting on the open fire.

Now, of course, a lot of Christmas nostalgia is, it might be argued, artificially induced. The commercial use of culturally established artefacts triggers warm feelings about the old days. It is hardly an accident that December shoppers walking around downtown department stores hear Bing Crosby's *White Christmas* or Dean Martin's *Let It Snow* but not Khachaturian's *Sabre Dance* or tracks from Rihanna's *Good Girl Gone Bad*. But why is such a musical invocation of Christmases-past just so repetitively potent?

Well, again the social norm effect is dynamic. Whatever the objective human reality of the holiday season, we all (most of us) do not want to be personally responsible for blocking the warm glow. Brand leaderships understand this all too well. It may well be that late December actually means spending time with family members we cannot stand; receiving presents offered in studied bad taste; eating foods we have hated since early childhood; watching movies seen so often we can do the dialogue before the actors; listening to songs so treacly that you could get a blood disorder from them . . .

But reality matters not.

Nobody wants to play the part of Ebenezer. Or refuse to wear a chunky red sweater decorated with an image of a beardy old man riding around the sky in a cart. Or to stick a burning hatchet on the snowman's head where the carrot would, according to convention, normally go. At Christmas time, things have to be wonderful. But the notion that *things-might-be-wonderful-but-not-as-good-as-they-used-to-be* becomes a wordless communal conspiracy. In twenty years time, it will be a majority of young Brits who are still telling researchers that Santa Claus used to be a much nicer bloke than he is now. Kylie Minogue's version of *Santa Baby*, that old favorite, will be heard in the background.

> "I love the old commercials especially around Christmas time when Santa was sledding down a hill on the electric shaver; those kind of things were fun and entertaining, really made you sit and want to watch it again. Commercials these days are not very catchy as they used to be".
>
> **Female, 47, mother, Melrose, NY, USA**

Life's good stuff—going, going, gone

In our Future Foundation global research program, we have, since this decade began, been asking people in two dozen diverse countries around the world some very direct questions about such stories in order to hear what they might say, to intuit what they might mean by what they say.

Let's consider this particular proposition for debate: *Too many good things from the past have disappeared.* Well, we find that around three-quarters of respondents in places as diverse as Brazil, China and the Czech Republic *agree* with the statement. For Brazil, there is barely any difference in the responses from those aged under-24 and those aged over-55. In China, we see a similar picture. In the Czech Republic, the figures are, in the widest sense, even more interesting still since well over 80% of those over-55 there agree while 62%—still a majority—of those under-24 take the same view.

These are, in each case, countries which have passed through profound transformations over the last generation. And we might well think that, to most of their fellow global citizens living in other parts of the world, such changes in the political and economic order of things would appear essentially and measurably benevolent. We may put the point too pointedly here but our evidence seems to suggest that even in places where history has so obviously shifted from a phase of political oppression or economic dilapidation (or both) to one of general improvement accompanied by the realistic hope of future success . . . so many citizens fret for all that has been lost in the fire of history.

We might well understand this if when we put such questions to consumer-citizens anywhere we do so in the immediate aftermath of a very recent, still totally front-of-mind unpleasantness. We think of the Credit Crunch. Or a particularly lurid political scandal. Or a dreadful flood. Or a sudden collapse in macro-economic growth. This could indeed lead to the kind of distortions of which all quantitative research is so easily guilty. (It is crucial, of course, in quantitative exercises of this kind to be sensitive to precisely *when* such questions are being put). But that really does not seem to be the vibe here. Whatever is objectively happening, millions of us equate the passing of time with a serious loss of value. This is sometimes referenced as the **Myth of Decline**. We use *myth* in two senses here: a compendium of stories (both distracting and informative) and a possible delusion (based perhaps on wilfully half-digested information).

Let's break to make a **Big Lie** speculation here. Most of us live in societies where tradition is valued as a kind of compacted wisdom. Important cultural artefacts like the Book of Common Prayer have changed little over the centuries as anyone attending a Christian wedding or burial service to this day will know. All religions have their sacred texts and many will be positively prelapsarian in both content and style. There have been 266 Popes in the Catholic Church, an impressive line of longevity going back to St. Peter. The prevailing Yamato Dynasty of Japan dates back—perhaps notionally but certainly impressively—to 660 BC. The wording of Presidential Oath of Office with the commitment to uphold the Constitution stretches back to 1789. In the UK, the national anthem is *God Save the Queen*, a song which dates back at least to the mid-18th century. In France, *La Marseillaise* was also born in the 18th century. Meanwhile, we passingly observe that the national song of Scotland, sung lustily at all major sporting events, is a mournful ditty about the fractious state of Anglo-Scottish relations in, yes, the year 1314. Over a large expanse of Latin America today, political discourse is often dominated by the concept of *bolivarismo*—a set of pan-continental ideas for governance and social solidarity associated with a Venezuelan politician who died in 1830. Again in France, so many of the principles of the civil and penal codes are eminently traceable back to Napoleon. Many countries have Founding Fathers or something such like; few countries have no defining, no *gubernatorial* book of constitutional genesis. Yesterday is such a source of not just ceremonial authority. As you walk around your life, you are walking through it all the time: so much cultural Dark Matter present in your rituals, your politics, your identities.

All this creates a significant hesitation within life psychology. It is not good karma to be too enthusiastic about the new. Consider how often, in modern history, social innovations are resisted or repudiated. Once upon a time, some thought that rock-and-roll was nothing less than a rampant subversion of moral order. Elvis, Chuck, Jerry Lee and all the gang were truly going to lead America's soul to bleed. Once upon another time, divorce—if you could get one in, say, Italy or Spain—was little more than a personal trauma and a social stigma. Not that long ago in some parts of the UK, it was virtually impossible to buy alcohol (or indeed anything) on a Sunday, the specially reserved day of the week. The celebrated anti-Marxist philosopher Karl Popper wrote a once celebrated pamphlet called **Television—Enemy of Democracy.** Back in the 1980s, the insight community of its day devoured Neil Postman's popperesque bestseller about the continuing dangers of television: **Amusing Ourselves to Death**. Television was herein viewed as a totally inadequate medium for sharing and analyzing complex ideas and therefore both a phenomenon and a behavior which would lead to intellectual and cultural despoliation all round.

Yesterday shines brighter than tomorrow . . .

In one of our Future Foundation trends—**Murdered by Modernity**—we monitor what we might call, in the present day, the *scholarship of imminent decline*. We reference here all those commentators who find evidence of fresh deterioration pre-ordained inside the very apparatus of way we live now. In the second decade of the 21st century, they especially complain about the various dangers of, say, spending too much time in front of screens (to the point of therapy-requiring addiction), making multiple "friends" on **Facebook**, thinking of online gaming as a "skill", relying on too much instant Googled knowledge and not learning things through proper dedication, failing to join community groups and acting as if the hours spent online constitute a fit and proper use of leisure time . . .

In the UK, there is a well-known neurologist—Professor Susan Greenfield—who has amplified a deep suspicion about the long-term impact of digital technology on our brains and our culture; like a number of other scientific contributors, she is concerned that too much internet will damage the cognitive capacity of children and possibly lead them to socially destructive behavior. In July 2012, the front cover of **Newsweek** magazine was an image of a very distressed-looking young boy under the headline *iCrazy. Panic, Depression, Psychosis—how connection addiction is re-wiring our brains*. Elsewhere in 2012—and we do not have to scramble for examples here—the front page of the **Healthy Active Kids Canada** report carried a picture of a dinosaur and was provocatively entitled **Is Active Play Extinct?** The report deprecated and plainly saw great danger in the fact that *"children and youth get an average of 7 hours and 48 minutes of screen time per day"*—against official guidelines which recommend only two hours per day. The US **Department of Health** makes a similar recommendation.

This big bad buzz is not hard to hear as the century has grown. Many an insight professional has read and wrestled with such now famous books and articles as Jaron Lanier's **You Are Not A Gadget;** Nicholas Carr's **Is Google Making Us Stupid?**; Lee Siegel's **Against The Machine: being human in the era of the electronic mob** . . .

And for French-speaking professionals and indeed parents there is, courtesy of Bernard Stiegler and Serge Tisseron, **Faut-Il Interdire Les Ecrans Aux Enfants**? (Should We Ban Screens For Our Kids?). Elsewhere one can feel this whole thrusting zeitgeist in books with titles like **Safe Text: protecting your teen from the dangers of texting**. Not that many titles, so it might seem, would say something like **This Whole Internet Thing—is it not all simply wonderful?** No, we are all going to hell in a hand-held device.

> "I can remember watching TV and waiting for the commercial. Back in the Fifties they were actually entertaining! Now all they seem to do is insult your intelligence".
>
> **Male, retired, South, USA**

Now, around 80% of both Americans and Canadians in our surveys agree with the proposition that parents should *limit the amount of time children spend using the internet*. This seems and sounds like a thoroughly responsible position, an adult response to some very powerful signals from public authorities, medical experts, paediatricians, etc. But pragmatically gathered time-use data will affirm that millions of kids across the Western world are being allowed by parents—including presumably those who completed our surveys—to positively devour the internet. Obviously, we offered an *Agree-Disagree* proposition to our respondents here which triggers a reply heavy with social norm. The value of such an exercise—and many like it—is at least to start to measure the gap between attitude and behavior in this area as well as to understand how parents might like to see their own anxieties (and failings?) treated by the relevant companies, suppliers and perhaps even public authorities. A perfect brick for **Big Lie** insight-building.

Meanwhile, there is not yet available to anyone, scientist or citizen, any real epidemiology of the internet *qua* threat to health. Back in 2000, it was still a minority of, say, Canadians and Americans who were real netizens. Saturation internet use is still a relatively new phenomenon across the Western world.

Of course, nobody would surely dispute that it is not prudent to fail to take regular exercise. It is irresistible that obesity levels really are too high, placing many individuals and, for that matter, many national health systems in long-term jeopardy. But why assume that public policy or self-induced social wisdom or even the sheer inventiveness of products brought to market by clever, socially sensitive and emphatically profit-seeking companies . . . would never do anything *ever* to address and possibly correct such pathologies?

The notion that *society-is-on-the-verge of serious-victimhood* from changes in its environment or indeed from the very creativity and inventiveness of human beings themselves runs like infinity police-tape through so much of the commentary, both scientific and populist, on the way we live now. It is as if in our history since, say, World War Two, no social problem has ever been corrected. How many of the direst dystopian predictions have turned out to be no more accurate (and no more threatening) than this month's astral confirmation of a new romance for those born under Virgo (as available in a dentist's waiting room near you)? The innocence of yesteryear always has to be teetering. Cassandra must speak. Doom, doom, I say, doom.

No soothsayer ever said: *You know what? It will probably turn out quite nice tomorrow.*

For now, specific anxieties about a possible and damaging re-configuration of the human brain resulting from all the doings of the Digital Age—leading to a higher incidence of disordered behavior—will be confirmed or confuted only after a long stretch of time. The authors of this book do not know if the opponents of modernity, some of whose stances are summarized above, will be proved right or half-right by events still to come and measurements still to be invented. Meanwhile, no sensible person would wantonly ignore media-borne warnings about such things from well-educated and well-meaning people. But, oh, how smoothly hyperbole hurries the voice of those who see decline in every turn of time's ratchet.

The future must be dangerous . . .

Down in the basement of all this, we can detect the presence of another trend—the **Culture of Fear**. In the opening of his book, **The Risk Society: Towards a New Modernity** in 1986, Ulrich Beck told us that: *In advanced modernity, the social production of wealth is systematically accompanied by the social production of risks*. Perhaps losing nuance in translation from the original German (**Risikogesellschaft**), this nevertheless comes over as an emphatically strange assumption. Note the implication that improvement in one life-theater must lead to hazard in another. But if risk is so penetrative and so permeable, then why are we all living longer in virtually every country on earth? (We appreciate that there is an ecological dimension to this story which we address elsewhere). So many intellectuals feel legitimated in acting as if, given the present we have now, the future is bound to be volatile, possibly explosively so and in ways not yet perfectly foreseeable. And definitely *worse*.

Arguments in favor of the Risk Society have had a huge influence across the world and certainly in business life. Much of Corporate Social Responsibility has, in the modern era, been seriously shaped by it. Consider the play of the related Precautionary Principle in the (self-) regulation of, say, the food and pharma sectors. One consequence of this is that the past seems infinitely more stable than the future. As Ulrich Beck himself says at one point:-

"The center of risk consciousness lies not in the present but in the future. In the risk society, the past loses the power to determine the present. Its place is taken by the future, thus something non-existent, inventive, fictive as the 'cause' of current experience and action. We become active today in order to prevent, alleviate or take precautions against the problems and crises of tomorrow and the day after tomorrow—or not to do so".

(Risk Society: Towards a new modernity. Sage Publications. Edition 2007)

In other words, as time passes, any exposure to danger and possibly disaster is magnified into potential reality. Every yesterday is bound to be safer than any tomorrow. Nostalgia thus receives extra intellectual validation as a scheme of thought and an attitude to life. Many might well contest the inner logic of Beck's position. But the notion that the future is, one way or another, bound to be intimidating makes a kind of running glory out of the past.

> "Of course, when I was her age, our biggest thrill was to get a 6 pack of beer. We didn't even think of using drugs, getting an STD, having our identity stolen or being stalked! We also knew we would be able to find a decent job somewhere that would lead to a company funded pension. The wealthy kids went to college, the rest of us graduated high school and went to work, but we all did OK. Children nowadays HAVE to get additional training after high school and they still may not be able to find a job. Also, they are going to be saddled with a ton of debt from the US government. Children today have it harder, much harder".
>
> **Female, 62, retired, Baltimore, MD, USA**

There is indeed nothing dramatically new, philosophically speaking, in all this. For, as we pass through this part of the story, let us notice just how regularly the very business of consumerism itself has been the target of complaint and suspicion.

Some authors from this stable have long since insisted, for instance, that as income growth has spread so millions face a befuddling frenzy of choice (so many types of orange juice in the store, wines now from dozens of countries, hundreds of product variations for the simple digital camera, more versions of the cell phone contract than there are, well, cell phones . . .)—to the extent that human contentment is menaced by constant instability.

It was in 2004 that the American analyst Barry Schwartz published his influential book with a famously self-explanatory title **The Paradox of Choice: why more is less**, a concept endorsed by many others then and since and often associated with the movement loosely known as *voluntary simplicity*. Further back in 1999, Juliet Schor produced her **The Overspent American: why we want what we don't need**. This was followed in 2004 by her **Born to Buy: the commercialized child and the new consumer culture**. These selections from the latter will give the drift of an argument that is still running through critiques of consumerism to this day:

> *"There are more than 46,000 shopping centers in the country, a nearly two thirds increase since 1986 . . .*
>
> *. . . According to my estimates, the average adult acquires 48 new pieces of apparel a year. She has also been discarding clothes at record rates, in comparison to historical precedents . . .*
>
> *. . . Heavy (TV) viewing has also resulted in historically unprecedented exposure to commercials . . .*
>
> *. . . Today's average (ie normal) young person between the ages of nine and seventeen scores as high on anxiety scales as children who were admitted in 1957 . . .*

. . . the typical American child is now immersed in the consumer marketplace to a degree that dwarfs all historical experience".

The thrust of such language is un-missable—and not at all uncommon in this strand of literature and comment. The modern age brings, by its nature, threats that are fresh and sharp. By comparative juxtaposition once more, wellbeing was easier to manage in the past. Everything there was better *a posteriori.*

Strangely, this literature of what we will too loosely call *preservational anti-consumerism* (with its illumination and condemnation of excess of all kinds) has prospered less in Western social analysis since 2008. Just not so many titles, not so much buzz, these days.

One assumes that our economic conditions are not propitious to such a thesis.

Let's take a moment to reflect further on this point. A serious implication for social and commercial analysis might be coming over the horizon here.

Consider our recent and prevailing economic fortunes. It is not hard to find evidence of just how supersize a bite the Credit Crunch (and all that followed hard upon) took out of people's pocket-books and prospects.

In late 2012, the **Bureau of Economic Analysis** in the US produced a particularly striking statistical retrospective: *personal income rose in 2011 in all of the nation's 366 metropolitan statistical areas (MSAs) for the first time since 2007"* (emphasis added). Back in the second quarter of 2000, US GDP growth cracked through the 5% ceiling and, after a bit of a blip around 2003, started growing again, often at a trend-respecting 3+%. Shortly afterwards, the economy was overcome with nervous exhaustion. After the headlong fall of 2009, the country found it hard to fix its growth machine. GDP growth was 2.2% in 2012. Not bad but . . .

Meanwhile, over the Atlantic, the UK suffered a double-dip recession: such growth as there was detectable by only a psychotically focused quantum mechanic. And the stresses of the Eurozone remain almost too gruesome to consider. Unemployment in regions like Extremadura in Spain can touch 30%—a plague on living standards and a lingering depression, one might assume, for pretty well every family there. Over in Greece, recession seems to run on a demonic loop resulting in, for much of the decade so far, a quarter of the workforce with no job. For its part, the Italian Government has, local conditions and international expectations being what they are, done little else except produce new austerity measures, fresh reductions in welfare, cuts in pensions, etc.

And so, truly does this not seem like a good time to be publishing books with titles such as:-

You Are Buying Too Much Stuff At The Shops, You Silly Greedy People!

Or **Smart Folks Go Without.**

Or **Happier When We Were Poorer: back to yesterday for a better tomorrow.**

The Big Lie lurks . . .

Our purpose at this point is to ventilate an oft under-remarked suspicion. As follows: there is indeed something of a contrived seasonality—a fashionability—to the content of academic or quasi-academic books/reports/departures about all the social and technological transformations through which we pass. Can we confront the possibility that scholarship, of the kind which interests us here in this chapter, might, at least sometimes, be being *produced in direct and exclusive correlation to the topicality of its specific subject-matter*?

In other words, is it what is *hot* that sells, just as much (maybe more?) as what is, in ways often subterranean and hard-to-measure, more profoundly *true*? The exploration that insight professionals must continually make about what is really happening in their societies and their markets—and what the future is most likely to bring—is quite easily blown off course by this very phenomenon. Given this suspicion, care must be taken. Detachment must persist. For there are some self-styled experts in social change analysis, often prolific and much reported, whom insight professionals should, under no circumstances, ever treat as authorities—and this for the very reason we raise here. If the intellectual has an angle or is just out there to ride a popular wave, he is not an intellectual any more.

And while we make the point, let us ask: Do you think that every famous business leader or guru has actually read the wannabe famous business book which he/she so lavishly praises? You know—the quoted recommendations you read on the back page of the bestsellers you browse at airport bookshops?

No. Neither do we.

Something of an irony is at work. A defining premise of our **Big Lie** is that in opinion research exercises, consumers do not yield the perfect truth about their lives, influenced as they are by what others think/what they think they ought to think/what they think the interviewer ought to hear from them/what they used to think they ought to think but actually think no more. And so on. Advertisers and marketers have to live with this obfuscation-filter and adjust to the challenge to their creativity which results. At the same time, intellectuals and analysts may sometimes offer only *versions* of the truth which are *partial* in every sense of the word. The culture of the **Big Lie** is everywhere.

It is striking, in this setting, how the one industry which rarely has any nostalgic interest in its own past is: forecasting. It is a surprisingly common practice for macro-economic forecasters, for example, not to refer back too often (if ever) to their old predictions. This is because so many of them turned out to be not very accurate or, in fact, hopelessly indeed almost pornographically wrong. In his book **The Signal and The Noise**, Nate Silver makes much of the psychological and professional pressures on economists to conform to certain analytical presumptions and points of view. He helpfully lists all the cognitive biases to which the forecaster's flesh is heir. One of the most striking implications of his review is, in our opinion, that economists can form a kind of mutually reinforcing and continuously self-referencing tribe. Under certain circumstances, it may well make sense—*within the tribe*—for one young member to make an outlandish prediction just to attract attention. Or, in the interests of collective protection, for all members to say basically the same thing out of a general fear of failure in particularly stressed circumstances.

Along the way, objective reality and the clinical pursuit of truth are eminently corruptible. Generally, our point here, the power of this intensity of professional consensus is such that it is just like the workings of social norms under the influence of the **Big Lie**. When we say things, when we respond to questioning, two voices, if not more, can often be heard by the attentive listener: what we think we believe or know and what we think we ought to say. At business, at home, at the shops, with friends, in life. More, as Nate implies about the whole forecasting industry, one can never make a perfectly objective prediction—for the prediction will always be tainted by our subjective point of view. (In our view, this is a bit pessimistic. Forecasting, in the sense of trends analysis, can become a higher calling by purposefully shedding some bad habits—a notion we address later).

And if you have ever heard of trends consultants predicting that **Diet Coke** would never fly; that celebrity culture was a transient fad; that social media would never be a majority sport; that nobody would surely ever want to take a photo of the chimichanga his girlfriend was busy devouring in a TexMex in Kansas City and post it on the internet; that a rental market for such things as designer handbags would probably never exist; that we were all about to hurt from a bad condition called *Box Set Anxiety*; that erotic novels would never go mainstream . . .

. . . then, well, you will not be able to find the original reports and studies these days.

For they are long since erased.

Everyone, consumer and consultant too, has a capacity for a creative manipulation of history: now you see it and now you do not. Memory-banks and performance-reviews can be managed, in the dead of night, in dastardly selective ways. Sorry if you are shocked.

We do not have to take an opinion about which voices might be more or less right about any one aspect here. What we notice is that change is always challenged and that departures from previous behavioral disciplines always questioned. In a way, one might think, we speak here of one of society's most enduring mechanisms.

These happy days are yours and mine . . .

There is an old Robert Duvall movie called *Tender Mercies*. His character, Mac Sledge, has a famous line. *I don't trust happiness. I never did. And I never will.* We might link such a remark to a commonplace of evolutionary biology: loss and regret sting more than gain and pleasure bless.

But before we dig into that idea, let's take Mac's remark as our text and riff briefly on the whole structure—the history, the purpose, the direction—of emotional well-being. Could the hand of the **Big Lie** be at work inside the expression of popular opinion here?

Might we hold this following truth to be self-evident?

That while we are likely to self-report that our level of personal contentment with life in general is high, we are also likely to hold the opinion that others are either not as happy as we are or not as happy as they used to be or both. It is essential to qualify that last phrase: **we are likely to tell researchers, when they ask us about all this, that there is less happiness around.**

> "I am 52 years old and have seen the subtle, but gradual decay of morality and this has led to a *do what I want, no matter the consequences to self or* others mentality".
>
> **Male, 52, social networker, Bentonville, AR**

Earlier in this chapter, we reviewed some public reactions in different parts of the world to the suggestion that: *too many good things from the past have disappeared.* Let's take the story forward now.

Across all age groups, it is a majority of Americans who affirm to our Future Foundation interviewers that: *The stresses of modern life mean that people are less happy than they used to be.* (Interestingly, around a third of US respondents neither agree nor disagree.) Meanwhile, the **UN Human Development Report** from 2012 (for a period hardly known as a bonanza of big bouncy optimism in the US) tells us that the majority of Americans report themselves content with their lives. On the UNHDR's scale of 1-10 (where 10 equals *very satisfied indeed*), the US figure is 7.2. And while we alight on this figure, let us mention that the equivalent for Australia is 7.5; Sweden 7.5; the UK 7.1. In all these latter countries too, it is again a majority who tell Future Foundation that: *The stresses of modern life mean that people are less happy then they used to be.*

Incidentally, it is around 60% of American under-24s who agree that: *too many good things from the past have disappeared.* In the same age segment, it is a majority who agree in Australia and the UK. The equivalent figure for Sweden is just under 50%.

We raise here a phenomenon which vexes many a social researcher. Self-reported happiness levels tend to stay quite stable over time while the prevailing sense that *people around us are more unhappy than they used to be* seems stays stable too. In an otherwise excellent and fascinating book called **Social Trends in America: Findings from the General Social Survey**—edited by Peter V. Marsden and published by Princeton University Press in 2012—the authors note that happiness levels in the US have changed little since 1972. They go on to suggest that such levels *should* have increased in concordance with an improved economy and the compound rise in living standards. This is on the principle that, by the evidence available, *richer Americans tend to be happier.*

But any quick-and-dirty application of the **Big Lie** theory would most certainly expose the presence and the danger of too linear, too programmatic a logic here. There just has to be a psychological limit to how much happiness even the richest person—even Carlos Slim, even Lakshmi Mittal, even the latest **Powerball** winner—will admit to having.

Consider this. If you have just won a big promotion in your company (a company where the competition for top jobs is savage and under-performers at any rank are promptly shed) do you really—whatever the extra income and benefits—feel more securely happy than before? Excited, elated maybe, especially after that nice flute of celebratory champagne? But *structurally* happier inside your bones?

Does life really work that way?

Unfortunately, it seems not.

How to measure human happiness/contentment and how to interpret what consumer-citizens tell researchers about how they are, in this sense, feeling remains one of the most controversy-laden themes in analysis, social and commercial. In Europe and across this decade so far, **Eurobarometer** (the public opinion service of the European Commission) reports that when Europeans are asked: *Are you satisfied with your life?* then steady and often substantial national majorities (often over 75%) will tick either *very* or *fairly*. (We add a codicil here. Perhaps not surprisingly, Greek respondents have been expressing much less satisfaction in recent years). All this in the midst of, variously, low growth, high unemployment, crises of sovereign indebtedness . . . lots of bad juju on the streets.

Now, as we think about all this and its meaning for markets and marketing, let's go back to **Eurobarometer** (Special 273 Wave 66.3) published in early 2007. This was a more buoyant, bubbly time when the phrase Credit Crunch meant nothing more than some bingeing teenagers being financially grounded after a tense encounter at the Bank of Mom and Dad. As such, it should serve well as a small analytical laboratory for a *what-happens-to-happiness* investigation.

That study records astonishingly high levels of happiness across the continent. The question wording is: *taking all things together, would you say you are happy?*

Some results: 97% in Denmark; 90% in France; 92% in the UK; 82% in Germany; 81% in Austria. Now, we know the EU economy was in better shape back then but still . . . Hans, Marie-France, Nils, Jeremy, Hanna, the recently burgled Leduc family from Chalon sur Saône, the McTavishes (all still surviving on welfare checks) from Easterhouse in Glasgow . . . was *nobody* in this Euro-midst just a *bit* stressed maybe? What about the well-ventilated incidence of depressions, major and minor; the scale of alcohol and drug addiction; the strains of broken romances and family disputes; the horror of losing one's job in one's 50s; the start of senile behavior in a much loved grandmother; all the whips and scorns of time . . . ?

Well, let's get down on this. Telling a stranger who happens to work for a market research company that you are *not* happy is a tough moment. For it can a) sound like an admission of life-failure that it is just too psychologically burdensome for you to make to the man in front of you or on the phone b) feel like the kind of disclosure which is, in effect, a betrayal of your parents, wife/husband, family or c) be something that would do nothing but reinforce your unhappy state once you say the words out loud.

All career-guidance mentors offer the same coaching philosophy for job interviews: be positive, show good energy and drive, put your self-confidence on display. It is not fanciful that, for survey interviews involving certain types of directly personal question, consumer-citizens borrow something of this very approach. Who among us is going to tell that stranger: *Yes, please tick: Very Unhappy?* The social disciplines we inhabit invite us to do no such thing.

Frankly, for most of us in whatever income segment, privately to believe that any bout of individual happiness is inviolate and impregnable will just not seem socially normal.

In spite of what I might say in surveys, will I really attend a neighbor's barbecue to tell everyone in conversation over a beer just what a glorious life I lead? *Oh, where do I start? Perfectly healthy, thrusting career, much loved by my handsome/beautiful partner, satisfying sexual relations three times a week, great kids, totally at peace with myself.*

It is just not done. (Well, not by that many of us perhaps). Striking such a pose is wantonly hubristic. It brings down natural ridicule from our social set. We are all taught by our tribes that, soon enough, life will *so* smack everyone in the face. And frequently does. Best wisdom lies in fear, as someone in Shakespeare says. Objective truths—revealing progress or retreat in any life, improvement or decline, genuine optimism or robotic pessimism—become very hard to unravel. The trend analyst's quest is bound in a nutshell herein.

But walking back to happiness . . . There is a rockface of literature for the insight professional to have to climb here. The imponderables are these. Is there really more of it or less of it now? Does wealth help or hamper? Was the past really warmer, sweeter than today?

Oh, Happy Day

This is what we think.

The research community will not veer towards trusting happiness any more than Mac Sledge or any more than consumer-citizens themselves. For the average social scientist, just how easy will it be to say out loud: *Yes, I can definitely prove that in this area of life things are definitely better than they used to be and will probably stay that way?*

Scholars still write scholarly books and produce scholarly reports about something called the "hedonic treadmill". It's an old song. Oh, we cannot be happy until we have a brand new **Honda Fit** in the driveway just like our next-door neighbors, Jack and Lisa. Or take a vacation in Tuscany like that couple we met at that barbecue. Or— whatever it costs—send our daughter to an Ivy League school next fall just like the smart folks do. This is, broadly defined, the theory of competitive individualism, a theory which says that happiness is impossible even under conditions of serious income growth. This is because consumers will covet their neighbors' ox right up to the point where the ox turns into a **Ferrari**.

Such an idea feels like the wisdom of the ages. But it is, in fact, hopelessly out-of-date and certainly inadequate as a tool for analyzing marketplace behavior or predicting consumer responses. Let us be daring here and argue that too much social research is, in fact, badly deployed and thinly veiled ethicism. Lots of society's analysts clearly do not like what is happening in their social environment, see deteriorations in their midst and want to highlight them in order to stop them. Nobody in his/her right mind would actually admire addiction or excess, wherever they appear. *Absolute* libertarianism— letting people do what they want and learn by consequences but not by (as those concerned would define it) nannying or bossy regulation—is not a popular school of philosophy these days.

Competitive individualism may once have been a measurable dynamic of consumerism and a useful tool for communications professionals in the evolution of business strategy. But in a world of relative plenty, a world in which consumer-citizens have never been more educated or have never had more means of taking rational approaches to their consumption choices—does the theory still cut it? Or is its continued presence in social analysis proof of another kind of mis-aimed nostalgia? The old, familiar social diseases are still for some, as it were, the best.

Out there, there are doubtless scientists who took their degree in the 1950s still talking about Steady State physics and the Big Bang that, in their then prevailing view, never was. And experts in Cold War Kremlinology are probably still writing books about the history of the imminent collapse of the Soviet Union. Similarly in business-relevant trends analysis, old propositions can be as easy to shake off as molasses on your palm. So many contributors keep sticking around to prove that their ideas are forever inviolable. The book-borne refrain *I-have-proved-once-again-that-people-cannot-possibly-be happier-these-days* is a popular one here. There is indeed still so much social enquiry dedicated to the conviction that widespread wealth is a pathology and that consumers are nothing but the dismal dupes of Don Drapers, old and new. For once upon a time in the good old days which nobody ever inhabited, only nice people sold nice things in nice shops—and never, ever invited us to buy, out of crass manipulation, something that someone else had just bought. A strange form of nostalgia indeed.

> "I am enough of a chauvinist that I try to buy American whenever I can even if I have to pay more . . . I try to shop at small stores in my area that are not part of a national chain. I bank at a small local bank. I buy at Farmers' Markets, local bakeries, local coffee shops . . .".
>
> **Female, 62, high school graduate, Baltimore, MD, USA**

You must remember this . . .

Of course, the past can be genuinely full of treasured emotional assets which are banked against time—even when these are somewhat mythologised. Your school days may not have been so much fun at the time but they seem like the yellow brick road itself now that you are working double shifts at a fast food emporium on the outskirts of Detroit or stuck in a marriage with no love left in it. Besides, nice things really do happen to lots of us and it is perfectly natural, now and then, to enter a cozy reverie about our first kiss, our first bike, our wedding day, that hole in one, that mad bachelor party trip to Rome when Jack pulled his pants down and a carabiniere kicked him in the Colosseum . . . Oh, how we laughed.

It is no accident that alumni organizations represent such a major source of income for colleges and universities. When the **University of Cambridge** in the UK raised £1.2 billion in celebration of its 800th birthday, one third of the money apparently came from former students. In fact, some 25% of registered alumni gave *something*. Across so much of alumni-directed fundraising everywhere, the *come-ye-back-to-your-youth* pitch is universal. Hear this website quote from the head of alumni relations at **Harvard**:

"It is the aim of the Harvard Alumni Association to see that your Harvard experience does not end at graduation. If you continue to be engaged with Harvard, you will find that your life with be vastly enriched. New horizons will appear and new friendships will form to match those that were a part of your life when you were at Harvard. You will feel the zest and excitement of your student days again".

If ever there was a market built on purified nostalgia, then the student reunion business is surely it. Harvard runs, so it appears, about 20 formal reunions every year and in 2012, the **Harvard Magazine** reported that the class of 1977 at its 35th reunion had broken the previous reunion gift record by raising some $69 million. Across the world, it is not hard to find examples of "alumni nostalgia nights" for local colleges of all sorts. In the wake of the Royal Wedding in 2012, the **University of Plymouth** in the UK invited former students to *tell us if you met the love of your life at university like Will and Kate* and requested a wedding photo for the files if things had gone that far. Some institutions are now gathering video interviews with students as they leave upon graduation (*What will you miss most? What are your craziest memories? What has been the best part?*)—thus building a stock of time-lapseable nostalgia assets (and fundraising collateral) for the future.

Yes, of course, we can all easily smell a cocktail of emotions at work in the human responses to all this. Some people might just want to catwalk their accumulated wealth in front of their quondam roommates and football buddies. (Philanthropy often comes wearing a loud shirt). But it is unmistakable in so much of the meta-narrative here that nothing yanks our chains as forcefully as the past. We are happy to make such donations just to feel we can be brought back in time, whatever our true experience of our own history. You may well have been a gauche, fumbling, homesick fresher who could not, no matter how much you begged, make friends even with the geeks and the nerds and the dweebs. But these days, you are the hero of your youth-dreams. Not for the first time in this whole story, it is not the objective truth of anything that really counts.

Meanwhile, the cult of nostalgia takes its fuel from the vitality of the instant archive, the swelling of online photo albums, the ease of connection and re-connection with friends old and new, the auto-logging of experience both profound and frivolous. The internet age is synonymous with data accumulation and intelligence retrievability. And it is a hearty incongruity of this age that never before have we all had more opportunity to *curate* our personal histories and that of our families. At the beginning of this century, when the world wide web was becoming just that, a new brand on the block like **Friends Reunited** could accumulate 15 million members—not exactly overnight but close enough. Though not the commercial force it once was, the brand is still trading on the theme of "Millions of Memories—all in one place" by providing an interactive space for personal material alongside official archives. **Facebook** is, of course, jammed with business alumni groups, resuscitated friendships, memory banks of all dimensions. Every bit of life can be pinboarded and kept forever. What, moreover, should we make of the whole idea of *faux vintage* photography and the devices which allow us to configure the present into historical imageries—a form of ready-mix, DIY, instant nostalgic-making? Past and present blur and seep into one another.

There are people passing through their teens now who, when they are in the sixties and seventies, will be able to revisit and re-assemble all that happened to them—probably for every passing week—during these years through which we now pass. Thinking about that prom night back in 2014? Well, in 2060, to entertain (sic) your family, you will be able to run the clips, do the montage of photos, bring back to life all the buzz and the gossip of that day—all while linking in real time to those still alive who were with you back then. Of course, it will all be delivered in technologies not yet with us. But we can surely all see the writing on the wall of time. For many, nostalgia used to be a combination of sentimentality and regret. Soon, for all of us, the past will be kept in color-coded lines on the surface of our retinas (if the retina function has not been by then outsourced to a Moon-based high-tech start-up called **an i for an eye.lun**). Nostalgia will be like our own personal department store, open all hours. And business will be permanently brisk. And, we predict, life in 2014 will all seem somehow better than life in 2060.

Of course, you do not have to look far to find some very stark examples of this whole story at work within the contemporary insight community and the imperative of insulating brands from estrangement from consumers.

In 2012, **Coca Cola** launched its **Share A Coke** campaign in Australia. The idea was to give consumers access, via creative use of a QR code, to a selection of popular songs from each year dating back to Coke's arrival in Australia back in 1938. This was so that consumers could be "taken back to a special moment that was shared and enjoyed by others" and could, if they wanted, post individual stories of why a song or a moment was especially important in their lives.

As we write, Honda is still running its **#FirstHonda** movement online, inviting customers to look back in appropriate sentimentality to the time when they bought their first car.

Not so long ago, **Dior** used an image of the actor Alain Delon from 1966 to relaunch its scent **Eau Sauvage**.

The **Kenwood** food mixer company's leaders say that they "proudly design and manufacture cutting edge, stylish and efficient kitchen appliances since 1947".

The **Warby Parker** eyewear brand makes much of the fact that its takes its corporate name from two characters in the writing of Jack Kerouac (Born: 1922).

One of the clothing ranges from **Levi's** carries this piece of glories-of-the-past hinterland: "Our source material is our own archive and our inspiration is the hardworking men and women that we have equipped for the last 140 years".

Examples are abundant. The nostalgic can indeed be used to sprinkle glamorizing stardust over the most mundane items and even (though we list no such examples here) some tired-looking brands.

> "More and more companies are giving their ads a 'homey' feel and a 'longevity' feel. Oreo Cookies is doing a campaign tied to their 100 Anniversary. Coca Cola referenced their "World to Sing" in their Olympic ads. I personally like it because it brings back a lot of memories".
>
> **Female, 62, high school graduate, Baltimore, MD, USA**

The essence of the nostalgia paradox . . .

But there is another side to this story, rich in **Big Lie** features. For it is a defining truism of commercial modernity that there will be certain propositions which, whatever else they can say about themselves, simply cannot invoke a glorious past—and consumers would be unbelieving if they ever tried.

Microsoft, a company which—let us argue it out loud—has altered the lifestyles of millions, has been with us only since 1975; **Apple**

came forth around then too. Not so long ago, the word *tablet* referred only to an Egyptian hieroglyph or a kind of soft toffee made by only Scottish Moms. Now the tablet is a portable dream-machine, a paper-light hand-toy with which to open the wonders of the internet at any moment and in any location. Our cell phones are cameras, alarm clocks, personal organizers, movie theaters, mirrors, roadmaps, shopping malls ... Consumers have never specifically asked for phones to turn out so multi-featured. In fact, if a trends agency had in 2000 asked a representative sample of, say, Scandinavians (a society with more early adopters for new communications tools than probably anywhere else) whether they would like a new phone which could double as a vacation camcorder then—we are certain—majority support would not have been forthcoming. Consumers can easily motivate themselves to presume, in surveys, in favor of simplicity and familiarity, in favor of the cozy and the well-worn. They will say they are ready to rebel against the onset of new complexity. But how easily have they been seduced away from such an attitude.

At the opening of this decade, Future Foundation asked people in the UK to respond to the following statement: *All I want a mobile phone [cell phone] for is calls and messaging.* Astonishingly, some 75% of our sample declared their agreement. The figure for the under-24s was 60%. At, literally, the same time, app-enabled mobile ownership in the UK was 25% and rising, with the penetration among under-24s already 45% and rising even faster. By 2013, smartphone ownership was touching 60% in general while, among the young, approaching saturation. Not for the first time in this narrative, we can measure a universalized instinct in favor of the simple life which lives cheek by jowl with a ravenous but under-acknowledged appetite for machines that can do all kinds of tricks. Thank goodness the inventors, developers and manufacturers concerned took little notice of what consumers *said* they wanted. Social norms, the herd mentality and even, on a bad day, the *wisdom of crowds* can have the perverse effect of suppressing the belief in progress and the products which make such progress irresistibly real. *Keep life simple* is a universal mantra. There is a famous Christmas song which at one point runs: *Does your Granny always tell you that the old songs are the best / And then she's rock and rolling with the rest.* For the consumer-facing trades, how true can the spirit of that lyric be. The consumer's first impressions, rooted perhaps in a collective fear of the new, often have to be flatly ignored.

Of course, it is hard for consumers—indeed it is not their job at all—to envision how technological inventiveness can solve the problems they did not know they had. How could a young father living in San Francisco just at the end of the last century know that one day there would be an electronic product, a device which would cause a bleep in his pocket if his teenage daughter had just, this very minute, deviated from her prescribed way home? Or that that daughter would have something called a safety app on her personal phone, a feature which would, if she ran into any trouble or threat, *alert a list of pre-ordained adults and send her precise location to them while automatically calling 911?*

Perhaps in the very near future, a pointed question to put to consumers in a survey will be: *Are you aware that your phone can also be used for making calls?*

The fact is that technological innovation makes progress a benefit and a blessing in our lives by regularly and wantonly *breaching* established public opinion and the social norms which are frequently held inside. Communities, as we suggest, huddle round conservatism; the longing for the old simple days becomes something of a group hug. How many of us adults, looking back, were ever made clinically and decisively aware that our phones were about to become computers? Would it have assisted the promotional efforts of the brands concerned if we had been? One rather suspects not. Often, the goal of creative engagement with consumers means noting, absorbing and bypassing—but, oh so crucially, not ignoring—what they say they believe.

Very soon, the rock-star stuff that is graphene and the marvels of nano-technology will make everything in our web lives ubiquitously available, bendable and foldable, with more storage space than a medium-sized city and more firepower than Apollo 11. The irruption of such fabulous communication, learning and entertainment tools— über-powered and hyper-personalized—continues to radicalize the lives of Mr and Ms Every-Consumer across the globe. On both the supply and the demand side, feature innovation is the age's drug of choice. If the heads of **British Telecom** and **AT&T** and **Telefónica** had ever got together in the mid-1990s in order to collectively ask their telephony customers what they wanted in the future what would they have heard in reply? *Just lower tariffs, please? Nicer operators? Easier access to engineers when connections fail? Smoother dialling? Faster horses?*

And yet, barely a generation later, if your cell phone is not capable of waking you in the morning with a hot cup of freshly ground coffee while automatically texting your plumber to call next Tuesday afternoon just after **All My Children**—then you feel deprived of basic life entitlements. Is anyone really nostalgic for the days when the family phone was in the den and you could use it only to make important calls when nobody else was around? Or when the only computer you could buy was heavier than a slab for the patio? Does any social media user long for the days *before* broadband was invented and available to all? Will there ever be a market for antique fax machines and old instamatic cameras?

Are the suppliers of the **MakerBot Digitizer Desktop 3D Scanner** and **Object24** or the rest of the additive manufacturing community developing their business model in direct response to the current state of consumers' opinion about the future role of injection molding in their daily lives? We think not. If we asked consumers how they felt about making their own designer shoes or children's clothes in the comfort of their garden shed, would a majority say that they would prefer to visit the mall and buy things in the way they have always done (and what a crazy idea anyway)? Most emphatically.

Given all we report in the earlier part of this chapter, it is strange to remind ourselves that the most powerful word in marketing argot remains *new*. Our whole culture has to self-neologize all the time.

Across the theater of their entertainments and communications, consumers crave the latest buzz, pounce on the latest tweet, upload an instant image of their freshest achievement, watch the newest dance craze video—in between all those work emails and all those *meet-you-in-the-bar*? texts. We exult in features and apps and options with an intensity that mocks the simplicity of our earlier lives. In days long gone, we might have swaggered to our friends about our new bike or the family's new sofa or Dad's new car. But the motion is different now. The expectation of permanent functional improvement is, these days, a social norm in its own right. Whoever *brags* about getting a new smartphone with loads of features? We can all get one.

To the extent that nostalgia involves repetition or replay so it is confounded by the mad innovation rush—and *rush* in both senses— that is the Digital Revolution. But essentially, both the analog past and the digital future compete for real time value in the consumer's head. And her responses to surveys and questions, both trivial and deep in content, reflect inevitable confusion.

Intuitions for Insight

- The **Big Lie** proposition is very obviously, very dramatically at work inside the consumer-citizen's attempts to approach, draw value from and generally deal with the past, personal and shared.
- There are conditions under which insight might well decide to ignore nostalgic feelings, however firmly and prominently expressed. Often consumers will say that yesterday's stuff was better, while buying and enjoying products that were invented only last year by brands younger than their teenage kids. Besides, the strongest sentimentality will often be reserved for moments that never really happened. The nostalgia endorphins will flow anyway—if stimulated well enough.

- Some markets (eg fashion, personal styling, home furnishings . . .) will continue to be able to use the past as recycled innovation, eg re-popularizing Sixties styles for young 21st century audiences. This will not change, no matter how technologically slick our lives become.
- People often live, it might be thought, in multiple versions of the present, past and future all at the same time—a string theory, as it were, for modern identity. A very substantial opportunity for professional communicators of all kinds is held inside this thought.
- More, some brands may, at certain moments in the commercial cycle, find themselves with little option but to talk about yesterday, how long they have been around, stirring consumers' happy feelings along the way. This might seem a spicier communications approach when economic troubles are deep and lasting. No message that says Things Are Getting Better All The Time is likely to *automatically* prosper— however much it might be objectively true that human progress is real.
- Surveys in which consumers self-report their happiness levels have to be read with the coldest analytical detachment. Once more, what they say that they think and feel is at the mercy of all kinds of pressures and conventions, which themselves may well not stay stable. The same is true for the values people say they affirm and embody in their lives. Is everyone as reconciled to, say, the realities of living in a multicultural society (and the spirit of tolerance which all citizens are invited/ expected to endorse) as they would tell others? Just how common *is* polite society? Is personal happiness always driven into being by the phenomenon of nice people having nice experiences? Do nobody's hands love dark?

- Scholarly interpretations of human happiness may say more about the scholarly interpreter than the true mental and emotional state of individuals and families. Even—perhaps especially—*experts* can hear what they want to hear.
- Nostalgia has been read as a force for conservatism, a hesitation in the presence of the new. It has to be a speculation that this will weaken over time as new generations come to expect, in the Digital Revolution, relentless creativity and change. But for now . . .

THE **BIG LIE**: USING THE STORY TO PUSH YOUR BUSINESS FORWARD

If something is dead, get it off your chest

It was on a Monday morning that the CMO came to call. She abruptly convenes a plenary meeting of Team Brand, Team Innovation, Team Futures and Team Sales. Attendance is compulsory.

She announces that she is bounty-hunting for new efficiencies across the business and is poised to cut budgets at any moment when she is no longer convinced that serious ROI is resulting from current spend.

In her review, she has totalized the sums (spread across the Teams) specifically spent on market research, qualitative and quantitative. She has already come to regard these sums as both financially substantial *and* strategically questionable.

And so, this morning, she has five questions to put to the meeting and wants an answer to each, here and now.

> 1. What is the relationship in our company between market research spend and the quality / success of innovation (new products, better service offers, sharper communication)?

2. Is what consumers are telling us about their lives, their tastes, their needs . . . being actively converted into competitive strength for our products and brands? (If so, how?)
3. By what means do we actually know when consumers are telling us the whole truth, the half-truth, anything but the truth?
4. If our budget for conversations with consumers were to be cut in half, in what sense, if any, would the company be 50% worse off?
5. Do those conversations ever genuinely contribute to the identification of new social trends, significant for the long term? (Examples please!).

Trying to make no sound as they listen to all this, Team Members suck their breath like Hannibal Lector. Frankly, if Dr L. himself were in the room rather than the CMO there would actually be less of a chance of a slow and brutal death. The Head of Team Futures feels as if a red-hot flipchart-marker has just been plunged into his breast. He just did not see this coming.

An hour passes. The debate rages. Colleagues elbow each other as they quickly draw charts and diagrams to show to their expressionless CMO. Some, more than sensing a bloodbath, start pinning their tale of blame on the donkey that is Team Sales (always the way in tense situations of this kind).

And then, the Deputy Head of Marketing, previously silent, takes the floor:

Look, Boss. I'm Lisa. I'm still new here. But I see where you are headed.

First up, everyone, let's all stop defending the past—whatever good it contained.

The fact is that the purpose of opinion research is to help us manage risk rather than gather knowledge. Well, I think so, anyway.

*If, for instance, our customers tell us that they are really concerned about global warming and carbon emissions then we need really sophisticated, endlessly updated ways of **weighing** that view—testing its impact against that of other concerns, assessing whether it is rooted more in social conversations than deep private motives.*

The way we use and manipulate market research data should drive the pursuit of this kind of revelation. When we do this, we justify our budgetary provision.

And when we ask about, say, upgraded service propositions across our product range, we have to work on the assumption that the customer always sees herself as the heroine of her own life—explicitly deserving an elevated experience in every theater. But we need to stay alert to the reality that she may demand something but not really want it and would certainly never pay for it.

*Many people, we should most emphatically assume, will want to be seen as more individualistic, more clear in their heads, more professional as managers of their lives . . . than they really are. The needs they actually want addressed by a company like ours may not only **not** be revealed by the answers they give to our researchers but may be positively occluded in that very process.*

Consuming is an ever evolving psychology just as it is an ever evolving economics. You cannot stick to what you all learned in business school a decade ago. Along the way, consumers are, inside themselves, very much in the risk-minimizing business too. It will be natural for them to express ideas that are well supported in their peer group and wider community.

Every time anyone completes a questionnaire or chats out loud at a focus group, that person is putting himself out there and his best self will have to be on display.

This means that that person will tend to drift away from extremes and into the center ground, just like successful politicians do.

How many individuals would tell a pollster that they are not really a very creative sort of person or that family-and-friends rarely pay attention to their views or that money is so tight at the moment that they would be happy to tattoo our corporate logo onto their butt if we could just cut our prices by 5%?

If all the great Renaissance artists were alive today . . .

At this point, Lisa's colleagues start groaning.

. . . they would be working as insight professionals, sculpting opinion data into beautifully shaped strategy. And art is deceitful above all things. The old masters always let you see what you want to see. Consumers cannot and will not paint portraits of themselves.

Our job, therefore, is to appreciate the real value of the half-truth and the real power of social conformity.

Our job is to repeat back to our consumers what they have told us—so that we show we have listened—while giving them in our products all that we conclude they, in reality, expect. Look at cosmetic surgery. If so few people say they want it or need it then why is the market booming all over the world?

Listening in this way is how—certainly in theory and in practice (if we get good at it)—we optimize innovation and perfect loyalty building.

We have no customers living alone on remote Polynesian islands. They all live in tribes, around one Bay or another.

So, my suggestion is to initiate an audit of . . .

The speech is interrupted. The CMO raises both hands in a gesture that says *Enough, already!*

She announces that she has much to think about and that the meeting is to reconvene next Monday at the same time. Everyone in the room has to re-attend. All the rostered agencies—advertising, public relations, trends, futurology, polling—are to be represented. A lot will be going down.

Let's consider some examples, drawn from the authors' real-life commercial experience, of how deploying the **Big Lie** concept as a mental filter, as an *auditing* device, can deepen the acquaintance with consumers and de-clutter the insight process.

Case Study One: Luxury Goods (alcohol, fashion, lifestyle accessories . . .)

China in Your Hand (How long can you hold it?)

A Western consortium of luxury brands from diverse sectors comes together. They want to discuss their connection with Chinese consumers; build interest in and affection for their products; create a psychologically robust platform for expanded sales in the years ahead; just generally share ideas about the market without spending too much money on social analysis.

So, what does our private polling tell us about the inner being of the emergent Chinese middle-class? Everyone in the consumer-facing trades knows just how enthusiastic these people seem to be for pretty well all the features and furnitures of modern living. They seem optimistic about the future facing themselves and their families; they crave premium goods from the USA and Europe; they are keen to travel, enjoy new experiences, let new tastes/sophistications into their lives.

But inside the hearts and behind the eyes of those interviewed in Shanghai, Jiangsu, Sichuan . . . what is really taking place?

Can we detect the presence of powerful social conformities and possibly creative exaggerations at work in the answers they give to researchers?

Do they occasionally (at least) contradict themselves as they range through their responses to all the questioning about the way China lives now?

And if so, what does this suggest about the frictions detectable in Chinese society and how they could be fruitfully addressed in commercial communication?

We start by assuming that the **Big Lie** thesis will assist in the interpretation of these consumers' dreams and help identify the ways in which prosperous Chinese citizens are genuinely different—*or not*—from their counterparts in California or in Kensington or in the Gironde? After all, no global brand wants to spend money running region-specific marketing or developing region-specific products when there is really more convergence than diversity in the attitudes of their customers.

Once again, the objective is not to start presenting "interesting" findings about the target community here. You can find such things in everything from the **Financial Times** to the **Wall Street Journal** to sundry trade-specific newsletters every day in life. As a 19th century intellectual figure still popular in Chinese political circles once said, the point is not just to interpret the world—the point is to change it. We have to listen to the data as much as we look at it.

How would we view, for instance, the following: the definition and the purpose of social success in contemporary China? We need to find an approach which can help absorb the surface exuberance of Chinese consumerism—with its frothy appetites for virtually all products and experiences—in order to pierce through to the irreducible truths which may lie below.

The analysis has to begin somewhere. So let's look at some apparent paradoxes.

We might start by asking what is to be made of the Future Foundation finding that **only 7% of Chinese women in our sample** *agree strongly* **with the proposition: "I like other people to be able to recognize the brands I wear"**. Around one third of those women agree *slightly*. But the most common response to the question is: *Neither agree nor disagree*. Over 40% of the female sample, in other words, simply refused to vote. Does this sound right to us as an expression of objective reality? Well, no. It would be unwise to start suspecting that a majority of prosperous Chinese women do not really care to parade their **Prada** and **Dolce & Gabbana**. We do not even begin to draw away from the presumption that this is a market and a society that positively exults in the display of personal economic success and cultural savoir-vivre.

But there are social inhibitions in the air. A *minority* of Chinese citizens, after all, have serious spending power.

From the many interviewed, a young woman in Shenzhen told us:-

"I hate those people armed up with excessive luxuries. Once I saw a lady wearing **Burberry** *glasses, coats, bags and shoes which makes me sick. Those who have good taste should only use one or two pieces of luxuries or even none".*

(Amid all the hubbub about imminent sino-domination of the global economy, it may be too easily overlooked that per capita spending power in the US is 5 times what it is in China. The income of an average rural household in China is 50% of that enjoyed by average urban household and, in spite of breakneck urbanization, around 50% of the population still lives in the countryside.

It can fairly be said that the majority—them that the Burberry-wearing lady notionally walks past on her way to the mall—are not yet sharing in the consumerist splendor that is portrayed every day in Western magazine articles and business reports about China today. And the silent presence of that majority presumably dilutes any tendency towards *to-o-o-o-o* much showy excitability among their wealthier cousins on the streets of Beijing).

From this preliminary data-moment we can being to sketch the possible limits to other forms of disclosure: in a time when public authority in Beijing is officially and emphatically against open excess or uncloaked hedonism, the political imperative merges into the social norm. Even to a *no-axe-to-grind* researcher, some truths are not to be over-admitted, whatever the explosion in ostentatious consumerism that so characterizes the modern Chinese middle-class.

Now, if we also ask whether our Chinese consumers enjoy following celebrities and what they are currently doing/wearing . . . then we find that *a majority of under-24s do not even put themselves in the **Agree** category.* And yet, famous young people like Yao Chen, Chen Kun, Zhao Wei . . . have a huge national following (over 40 million each) on **Weibo**. The actress Bingbing Fan is, as we write, probably the hottest celebrity in China and her presence and her image are relentlessly used to sell movies, fashions, accessories, philanthropic initiatives . . . all over the country; she has a formal promotional role, for example, with **Louis Vuitton** in China. The Chinese Ministry of Culture may try to ban some of her songs but Beyoncé can still pack a stadium in Shanghai. We do not require a list of too many examples here. We can readily embrace the living reality that celebrity is as throbbing a cultural engine in China as it is in California. But there is a clearly a widespread inhibition modulating popular acceptance of this.

We take a final example. Only 5% of Chinese middle-class women *agree strongly* that they would personally consider non-invasive forms of aesthetic surgery (such as Botox). With some justification, one has to see this as a brow-furrowingly low figure. We know from market data that the beauty and beautification industries are exploding in China. According to **ISAPS** in 2011, the total number of non-invasive procedures carried out in China is now just over 25% of the figure prevailing in the US. This is a market which barely existed in the People's Republic only a few years ago. Given China's population, it is right to expect that it will be, soon enough, the world's biggest market for skin-tightening products. Botox is the new rice.

Now, for all the above examples, Chinese respondents are actually still more openly enthusiastic (about putting, for instance, their fashion choices on display or wanting their faces re-configured) than their American or European cousins. It is their reluctance to be *even more* honest about what they really feel and the obvious presence of powerful social restraints on their responses to questions which fascinate us here.

In any exploration of this kind, it is essential to find both a philosophically sound and practically exploitable way of considering *all* the answers made by consumers to conventional questioning about their preferences and attitudes. Each response has to be put in a general context, a model wherein hyperbole might be diminished and any sense of socially imposed restraint might be weakened. The clients for the output in this project need to learn insightful things about how to position their cosmetics brands, present their jewelry pieces, invite drinkers to look upon their newly re-packaged whiskies as simply indispensable lifestyle accessories . . . in order to expand and protect profits in a society that is changing with every spin of the earth.

They do not want to be told by their commissioned consultants that 50% of the wealthy people living in littoral China apparently think that it might be a nice day tomorrow.

This imperative leads us into the realm of Globally Adjusted Data. In the version used by Future Foundation, this approach brings together the year-on-year results of our quantitative questioning in around 30 countries (with the same questionnaire taken into the field in each country). The task is to find national patterns in the way questions are answered—looking for the play of social inhibitions or the presence of exclusively local assumptions about commercially pertinent issues (price sensitivity, concerns for personal security, money worries, decision-making in the household, sources of advice and influence . . .). The result is national data deliberately managed to dilute exaggeration and to detect restraint—getting a truer picture into play. With enough questions being asked, it is possible to sense what is an average level of national agreement to consumption-related questions of all kinds—to sense what consumers will *tend* to say—and to thus recalibrate individual replies to specific questions.

For example, if 20% of American consumers say that they are interested in possibly procuring the services of, say, a personal lifestyle coach while the equivalent figure for our Chinese respondents is 75%, we would not necessarily assume that a) the figures represent the actual strength of the opinion in favor of such a service in each country or b) the gap is such that for every four Chinese consumers who have an appetite for the idea there is only one American. Under the mechanism of Globally Adjusted Data, the US figure will rise at least a little and the Chinese figure come down probably more than a little. In any international project of this kind, when a lot of decisions and investments ride on the best approximation of inner human reality one can find, the numbers sometimes need to be *curved* in this way in order to be brought into sharp focus. GAD acts as a corrective to casual expressions of the **Big Lie**.

This point in place, opinion research findings have to be activated inside appropriately insight-laden trends. The project output boils naturally down to a shortlist of these, trends which frame the future of Chinese luxury consumption. Without trends perspectives at play, one just gets buried under numbers, hypnotized by the carousel of charts.

One of these is the portmanteau trend **Vogue-Alization**. The trend postulates that the power of the global fashion industry, originating as it has in the West, creates shared cultural norms and expectations so powerful that they are, with localized variations (but not subversions), accepted everywhere in the world. The proposition is that the definition of personal beauty and public glamour is universalized. Fashion may also in this sense be seen as a way of disseminating what we might loosely call the values of a Western liberal outlook (social acceptance of beautifully dressed and even slightly dressed women, respect for different ethnicities, acceptance of different sexual preferences, concern for the welfare of animals . . .).

Now, such a trend, nourished as it will be by as much appropriately filtered qualitative and quantitative research as is considered necessary, cannot tell insight-hungry brands the full story. Many factors are influencing the evolution of luxury consumption in China as the century progresses. But **Vogue-Alization** is a device for *weighing* those factors and for creating a scale of comparability for different national markets. Are there conditions under which prosperous Chinese consumers would turn against American/European brands or start seriously to question the price premiums paid to acquire them? Is it possible to discern any shift in the definition of female beauty, a shift away from a look dominated by white skin and Western styling?

Once more, such speculations open the project rather than conclude it. But much is learned as the process outlined here grows into an early warning system for brands who know change is coming and who need to know how to ride it.

What did the project deliver?

- **An explanation of the limits to open and truthful comment about the pleasures of luxury consumption among those in the target segment.**
- **An approach to quantitative analysis which screens out the hyperbolic opinion and identifies the probable nature of the majority view.**
- **A sense of the trajectory of consumer culture in the market under review and a weighing of the options for initiative-taking by individual brands.**
- **A highlighting of the trends which, if applied judiciously, give the greatest possibility of building successful and sustainable intimacy with consumers.**

Case Study Two: Public Services (healthcare, schools, transport . . .)

Are People Sometimes Worth Under-Estimating?

A global accountancy firm wants to explore how consumer-citizens will respond to new ideas for the provision of public services (healthcare, transport, schooling, etc)—perhaps involving private suppliers rather than the established delivery mechanisms. The consequence might well be a cafeteria: basically, those consumer-citizens who can pay extra will be offered premium services from their governments. Not a two-tiered system but multi-tiered. Has this got a chance of flying?

To begin the project, the question is asked: *What do we know of public opinion on a subject such as this and should we commission a fresh wave of market research in the regions that concern us (the Americas, EU, Pacific Rim . . .) in order to road-test the acceptability of the whole idea?*

Now, unless there is some significant public relations dimension to the project, the consultant's advice in relation to the second part of the question should be *not* to invest in new research. This is because it is unlikely that new spend will achieve results that are analytically or commercially more valuable than what already lies, waiting to be mined, in publicly available material. Of course, if it is thought necessary to give the old parts of the story here a fresh lick of paint (ie via a specially executed questionnaire), then let's go for it. But we already have the ingredients to make the cake. Why waste money?

So, how do we start building the useful narrative?

With some foundational assumptions . . .

- Wherever incomes are rising or are (comparatively) already high, this will not translate into a swelled willingness to pay more tax. In fact, just the opposite is likely to be true: higher taxes will be deprecated.
- Public services are exposed to something like *infinity-demand*. Taxpayers already expect continuous improvement in service provision—a provision they will often regard, whatever the objective circumstances, as currently inadequate.
- Any discussion of this kind will inevitably provoke into play the public's attitude to and probably contempt for national politicians whom it will be thought, whatever the reality of their problem-solving performance, are shallow, dishonest or just randomly contemptible.

- Any experiment of the kind envisaged (*pay-more, get-more*) will have to be launched—if it is to be launched at all—without any definitive prediction of its success being feasible. In other words, prevailing public opinion will obfuscate rather than illuminate (unless it is analyzed through the prism of the **Big Lie**).

In countries like Mexico and Brazil, according to a source such as **Latinobarómetro** (2011), only about 15% of the population agree that income is distributed *evenly* in their country. The same source informs that more than three quarters of Mexicans and Brazilians are ready to declare themselves "satisfied with life".

In the whole of Latin America, meanwhile, more than 70% of people are equally satisfied while barely 50% agree that paying taxes is something someone has to do if he/she wants to be "considered a citizen". Only around 20% of the whole continent "trusts political parties" and around one third "trusts local government".

Even with snapshot figures like this, it is maybe not hard to tell what you *can* tell and tell what you *cannot* tell. For example, the worries that are expressed about poverty are significantly not sufficient to drown the personal contentment of the majority. More, virtually nobody south of the Rio Grande is going to say to a researcher or even a friend that he trusts the public authorities of the day to innovate into being clever new ways of delivering good schools or better medical treatments—or will give fair wind to any such innovation when it arrives.

But all this iteration does potentially begin to improve the quality of the *guesses* one can make about likely public reactions to the *pay-more, get more* concept.

Could it be that there is just no prospect of triggering civic engagement if the invitation comes from the political class? Or could it be that socially prevailing assumptions about politics and policy innovation represent the crust rather than the core of consumer-citizen opinion? Were the federal authorities in, say, Mexico to radically reform the **IMSS** and the **ISSSTE** along the lines of *pay more, get more,* is it possible that public opinion would start hostile and stay hostile without making any long-term difference to the ultimate viability of the idea? In other words, the scheme might be successfully run with millions not loving it but simply accepting it.

Clearly, the project begins rather than ends with questions like this. Doubtless the appreciation of the **Big Lie** dimension would be influenced by wider socio-economic considerations from region to region (prevailing size of the state, tax take qua proportion of GDP, income levels, quality and cost-competitiveness of the private sector offer, public expectations of state subsidy . . .).

For the **Big Lie** would, on its own, hardly allow the full, insight-bearing picture to be painted. But the approach it embodies should clarify the essential strength or shallowness of the opinions of those who are the putative beneficiaries of policy change. And this unmistakeably creates the basis for more accurately targeted messaging were policy innovations of the scale envisaged ever to be launched in the future.

What did the project deliver?

- **A framework for understanding the potential softness and malleability of public opinion**
- **An appreciation of where continental or regional differences mattered and where they did not or might not**

- **A prediction about the likely welcome for serious innovation within the policy spheres under review—whatever citizens say in interview**
- **An invitation to spend less rather than more on new research**

Case Study Three: Energy (oil, motoring . . .)

Does the wind sit in the shoulder of your sales?

The futures team of a major supplier of oils and lubricants with operations all over the United States is seeking to define what will be driving regulatory intervention in their market over the next five years. What do they need to know? How do they need to think? Under what foreseeable conditions should they *act*?

A number of possible *agents of change* have to be interactively considered:

- Public concerns about environmental despoliation and the degrading of the natural world
- The priority given to environmental questions by contemporary politicians
- The impact of eco-lobbyists and the impact of their choice of campaigning issues
- The pressures on personal car-based mobility: the result of traffic congestion and policy responses to the problem at the state and city level / issues of personal in-car safety and the pursuit of accident reduction

The desired output from such a study is an identification of the steps that the company ought to consider taking in its own long-term interest. Steps relating to:

- Product improvement and innovation
- The maximizing of customer support for whatever new eco-initiatives the company feels it necessary to take
- The development of optimized relations with public authorities, state and federal
- The search for first-mover advantage over marketplace competitors
- The protection of market share across all sectors and sub-sectors

Now, even though pretty well all citizens will have opinions about the quality of the cars they drive, the experience of motoring for work and leisure, the daily costs of getting around . . . it is right to envisage that most can contribute *but a limited amount* to the futurology that such a project entails. Not that many people follow the detailed programs and positions of **Friends of the Earth** or **Greenpeace** or, for that matter, the **AAA**. For this reason, expert opinion has to be summoned. Specializing academics and industry commentators are asked to supply views on the trajectory of regulation, point by point, issue by sub-issue.

Now, the working assumption has to be that the **Big Lie** never sleeps. The answers that come from experts have to be screened too. Norms and conformities can inhabit the views of professionals just as much as they characterize the responses from consumer-citizens to a pollster's everyday questions. A specialist commentator can mean well but still have an angle. He is generally not programmed to say: "I'm not sure". Or "I have completely changed my mind about this issue in the last couple of years". Or "Professor Mander over at UCLA knows so much more about this question than I do".

Of course, it is extremely valuable, indeed crucial, to those running a project with such an agenda and such an ambition to hoover expert opinion right onto their charts. The intellectual muzak surrounding a particular theme (such as, say, the future of oil dependency in mainland USA) has to be captured. Amid this, it is quite possible for one specialist to carry serious influence over the development of public policy even when a) his arguments are not verifiable and b) he holds opinions that would be repudiated or only part-endorsed by others.

We may even dare to suggest that some academics often try to build personal repute by deliberately looking for and amplifying points of disagreement with the prevailing orthodoxy. Has anyone ever read an article in a scholarly journal (Psychology? Medicine? Politics? Marketing?) which is subtitled "How I ended up agreeing with what everyone else has said so far"? In an interview, the professor can pursue creative differentiation for himself just as sedulously as a consumer does. The **Big Lie** filter-gauze has to be wrapped around every comment, every contribution, from whatever source.

(One might want to think here, for a metaphor, on the cacophony of claim-and-contradiction that has exploded among expert economists since the Credit Crunch and the fall of **Lehman Brothers**.

Financial regulation was too slack / should have been slacker.

All the fault of the Federal Reserve / all the fault of the big bankers and their big bonuses.

*The downturn was foreseeable (and **I virtually alone** foresaw it) / was predicted only by those economists who habitually predict recessions every six months (bound to turn out right one day).*

The solution is a massive stimulus plan / is a brutal reduction in the national deficit.

Tax cuts will do good / do terrible harm.

I nearly got it right / did not quite get it wrong).

Now, in the case of our project, the experts—academics, journalists and former departmental officials—do real good. They are especially informative about international trends in traffic management and tax regimes relating to car mileage— suggesting that so many trends in this area can show a significant *velocity of global transfer.*

In other words, no matter what is officially the national scope of the project, it is very fruitful to open it to non-national narratives. This means noticing what shifts in the direction of public policy are taking place in, say, Scandinavia or Singapore and which commercial initiatives seem to be doing well in ways which could easily be replicated here. For the future of regulation, agents of change many indeed exist outside the US, potentially influencing American lobby groups, politicians, journalists and commentators and even—in some cases, at least—household opinion.

So far, so good.

Of course, one major, multi-layered question emerges as the project nears its climax. Is the condition of public opinion such that:-

a) *Americans are broadly prepared to welcome restrictions on personal mobility if the environment is the beneficiary or if other improvements are the corollary (better public transport, less congestion . . .)?*
b) *Americans may offer what would in some quarters be regarded as progressive views about the need for more regulation of personal transport but would in practical reality resist or even revolt against any such moves?*
c) *Americans are generally hostile to greater regulation but i) are likely to grow less hostile in the years ahead or ii) are likely not to change their opinions much?*

In other words, just what space is going to be yielded to the ambitious policy-maker or even the innovation-taking company from within public opinion?

Let's face it. The issues involved are truly very hard for the ordinary family to ingest. It is no wanton disrespect to expect that public opinion will be a jambalaya of impulses, contradictions, social conversations, personal experiences, things read in newspapers, political inclinations . . .

What, for example, are we to make of our finding that around **90%** of sampled Americans will **not** endorse the statement: "I do not see the point in being environmentally friendly because I do not think my personal actions are going to make a difference". Most people like to express a measure of eco-sensitivity, like to be seen as eco-aware. And yet, around 40% of Americans, when given a list of things they could putatively do if they were wealthier than today say that they would buy a new or an extra car.

As one of our focus group contributors in New York said to us:

"People make a connection of extreme weather with climate change but not directly with their behavior or choices like having a car . . . which is sad".

Another said:

"Climate change is starting to seem like a reality and I think people want to act on it but don't really know how".

Only a minority of Americans tell Future Foundation researchers that they now think that renting a car for short periods /specific purposes is preferable to owning one outright. Federal statistics (**EIA**) reveal that car sales in the US will continue to rise all the way to 2040 and that—with Credit Crunch blues now something of a yellowing snapshot—vehicle miles traveled per driver are due to increase *each year* from 2014 to 2040. For comparison, VMT is 11,980 in 2014 and will be 13,280 in 2040.

(At this point, we re-introduce the standard Future Foundation codicil. We remain unalterably hesitant about long-run linear predictions bearing very precise numerical values. We use some here, in spite of ourselves, to indicate, so to speak, a general direction of travel. But the notion that there is no reason to expect that conventional driving will naturally decline would be readily endorsed by our own trends analysis. That much we can say).

So far, no great revelation here. The generality of Americans continues to want the maximum personal mobility at the lowest prices and with minimum interference on lifestyle choices—but without wishing to seem too insensitive to the need for controls over that mobility.

All this gives rise to a special speculation, one to be brought into the heart of the project's conclusions. *The greatest source of influence over public opinion and personal behavior will be product and service innovation rather than anything else.* Just as people and policy-makers fret about congestion on the freeway, the warming in the air, the price of gas, the impossibility of finding a nearby parking lot . . . so highly inventive offers are jolting expectations and behaviors alike. So many people who answer questions from researchers may still be thinking—hardly their personal fault—in entirely 20th century ways. Expressions of the **Big Lie** may speak of a time which is already being superseded.

What are we meaning here? Apply a trend like **End of Inefficiency**. This is a proposition that in market after market the consumer's discretion is voluntarily suppressed as he/she is able to reap the benefit of intelligent systems: for example, a device which automatically switches your home utility supplier to the company offering the lowest tariffs this season or which, without needing to refer to you, transfers your savings account towards the best rate of interest. It is quite clear that, for its part, personal mobility is tracing a similar evolution, indeed revolution.

Autonomous cars plus freeway convoys plus devices which can navigate via the optimized route to that free parking spot (and reverse into it with no human hand on the steering wheel) are already with us. Terrain-sensitive vehicles can also adjust to hazard and reduce speed to avoid accidents and scrapes. All manner of in-car innovations have already reduced driver involvement and increased the likelihood of reduced energy outlay. According to the **EIA**, there are already over 11 million alternative-fuel vehicles at work in the US. The fuel economy of LDVs, meanwhile, increases all the time.

In so many policy-relevant directions, this is a sector where changed behavior and desired outcomes are not so much a question of policy intervention as an expression of the sizzling power of technological innovation. Once upon a time, economists would recommend using price incentives to stimulate a different kind of conduct on the part of consumer-citizens. For example, in Europe, sales of unleaded gasoline were once driven forward from an invisibly low base by a tax regime which disadvantaged the conventionally leaded alternative. The improvements which those responsible for the regulatory environment in the US might well wish to see (much improved fuel efficiency, weakened dependence on imported oil, more easily managed inner-cities, enhanced citizen safety, greater exploitation of renewable energy supplies, a higher standing for the US as a green economy in global league-tables, fewer cars journeys with no passengers . . .) can be driven as much by new business start-ups and new apps and new mobility services as by any other force.

The oil client has to continue to cock an ear to what its customers a) say out loud and b) actually think. But it grows clear that the nature of the welcome those customers will give to new regulatory initiatives is a function of supply-side factors over which they have no control and which, in so many cases, could not possibly see coming.

(One day soon, a nervous man will drive his family on vacation to Oregon; he is nervous because for the first time he is going to be taking his **Honda Fit** to join a freeway convoy which, thanks to the electronic wizardry emanating from the lead car, will allow him to take his hands off the wheel and his eyes off the road ahead for some 200 miles. Once the journey begins, however, he settles down to sharing coke and sandwiches with his wife and kids. For an hour or so, they watch the latest from **DreamWorks**. Back from vacation, he tells his friends how easy he personally found the adjustment to this new driving style—his pre-match anxieties recalled but not voiced).

The point is that in an analysis of this kind it indeed remains vital to track what consumers say and crucial to put their responses inside a working model of socio-economic and technological change. The **Big Lie** approach can help isolate the real motives and anxieties which sensitive brands have to address in their communication. This done, the ultimate role that public opinion actually plays in the evolution of the subject under review—the future of regulation in the human transport sector and the opportunities facing a major market player as a result of that future—can be properly assessed.

What did the project deliver?

- **An appreciation of the extent to which the feelings of the public actually shape policy and regulation.**
- **The role of such eco-sensitivity that exists in distributing responsibility for pro-environmental action across policy-makers, publics and corporations.**
- **An isolation of the ideas and interventions, from whatever source, most likely to produce changed human behavior.**
- **Advice on what any one company could actually do to win competitive advantage in the conditions described and given what the medium-term future actually holds.**

The best laid schemes . . . might actually work

Time to cut a new agenda

The CMO begins to address the reconvened meeting.

I have been thinking about what Lisa said last week. Moreover, I have spent a lot of time, often into the wee small hours, re-reading my own notes about things. I am talking about everything from competitor analysis reports, our own consumer satisfaction survey findings, the recent track record of our product launches and re-launches, our retail sales performance . . . You have a pack of the relevant documents in front of you.

Things need to change around here. For no-one could really answer my pointed but obvious questions when we last met. So I have a lot to feed to you in this presentation this morning.

*I am looking not just for efficiencies. A streamlined strategy does not necessarily mean a haircut for headcount or compressed budgets. But I **am** going to isolate every and any point in our processes at which we can no longer validate what we are doing or at which we miss opportunities that other brands on our block might well be getting ready to exploit.*

We are active in a wide range of consumer-facing sectors. For our presence and our prosperity inside those sectors, only insight keeps us strong—insight about how our customers (and those who are not yet our customers) are living their lives under all the trends shaping our country and our marketplace.

As you know, around 75% of our business is done here in the US. We make sales in every part of the Union. The rest take place across the world via our affiliates in Europe and Asia. If so much as a dead leaf falls into the backyard of any customer anywhere, causing a hardly noticed distraction in their thoughts, then we want to know about it. Though our brand managers are focused on those customers, those customers are not, from hour to hour, focused on our brands. We need to share their perspective. We are but furniture in their lives. And it is in the undercurrents of those lives—the casual opinions, the stresses, the conventions, the need to belong, the boredom and the reverie, the self-delusions, the hopes for better things—that we do our prospecting.

Too often, our opinion-gathering has been repetitive, conservative, lacking in daring, lacking in sensitivity, lacking in creative analysis.

In the end, I am not here to run a self-serving bureaucracy, with staff interested only in pay-checks and pension-plans. I am here to run a team that gets its kicks from shredding the competition. All real rewards flow from that.

So, the new culture . . . or . . .

Now that is what I call Big Data!

Yes, we want to know how consumer responses to certain propositions might be changing over time.

For example, if we have asked over the years how our customers define luxury in their lives then it makes sense to keep checking this. What was a treat or an indulgence for the average family a decade ago might be an everyday, throwaway thing now. In this and in everything, we have to keep a grip on the big, the shared narratives running through modern life. If there is a conversation taking place which carries consequences for how our people shop, then, to put it crudely, we need to be bugging it.

For instance, take the past. Can we make a priority of learning whether our people out there in consumerland want to talk more about the good ol' days now that America maybe seems a more divided place in this era? Yes, we can. This is very much the kind of issue we should be tracking.

The trouble is that we have in our standard questionnaires and focus group briefs too many badly drafted interrogations. We have been taking into the field repeat-questions year-on-year which were not good enough when they were first introduced back in the day. By "not good enough" I mean hopelessly underpowered and, at worst, downright confused. We ought to be using opinion research to penetrate all the important social conversations of our time—the conversations which reveal the general attitudes and direct the granular behaviors of our customers.

From now on, I will personally sign off all questionnaires and briefs before they are taken into the field. Every superfluous word will be excised.

And let me tell you something else at this point.

Some of you may have got it into your heads that we are all becoming, let's call it, slaves to the algorithm. From the stories in the business press, you may be assuming that the explosion of personal information-harvesting is transforming the nature and the value of insight. Big Data, so some might think, will drive out all the old ways of listening to and talking to customers. Customer-tracking and trend-anticipation thus become a mechanism, a mathematics rather than an art or a skill.

The promise of Big Data is that we will soon be able to identify and manage people as individualized bundles of trends rather than samples and segments. So, what will be the point of talking to people so much if we already know how they are going to behave? If we have so much back-story, why will we need a front-story, a Q&A, at all? Think of all that banked-up, back-down-the-years intelligence about purchase histories—all the movies we have ever bought, all the authors we like, all the skin creams we prefer, all the vacations we have taken in Florida, all the sums we spend on gifts in the holiday season each year, all the diets we attempt, all the cold remedies we give to our kids year after year . . .

Yeah, Big Data rocks alright.

But when I am the CEO of this company, we will still be questioning consumer-citizens in the way we do now—with the only difference being that we will be doing it better than ever because we will have intuited and absorbed the very best analytical techniques and styles along the way.

And when I stop being the CEO and one of you takes my place, we will indeed be doing all this still.

Why?

Because a company like ours that operates in a vicious competition for share will always need to know **why** consumers say things and want things and buy things.

We will always need to know **how** they might be beckoned—whatever they say in their surface dialogue with us—into changing their shopping practices or switching brands. We will still want to measure the impact of influence on their lives—the influence of socially spreadable ideas, the political discussions of the day, what their parents told them, what their buddies buzz about . . . Big Data is not going to stop people having an inner life, that private place **where what they say about things** to their families or to researchers may well be confounded by other thoughts and instincts.

And if big numbers are so smart, how come **Lehman Brothers** no longer exists?

Their spreadsheets once confirmed to the suits on Wall Street and in the City of London that it was proper business to loan money to folks living in trailer parks in order that they could buy five-bedroom suburban townhouses. Consider all that happened after that.

Have you ever wondered why the **Federal Reserve** keeps getting the big economic forecasts so spectacularly wrong?

If we can explain the whole of life in figures, does this mean that we can really anticipate which brands in a particular market sector will prosper?

*Take an instance. If a movie star launches his own range of flavored tequilas tomorrow, then how could the commercial success of the initiative be mathematically modeled **before** drinkers start to consider the reasons or even the non-reasons, the **irrational** reasons, why they might fancy buying the new liquor and offering to their friends at home? Arithmetic can never drown discretion or whimsy.*

*I know we are all bored with **Fifty Shades**. But who out there predicted that such erotica would become **so** massive, **so** suddenly? Who foresaw that the President of the United States, no less, would be asked about a book of that genre live on Oprah? Or that the book concerned would be translated into every major language on earth? Yes, data fiends can track **how** the momentum for the product built slowly on the internet and how smoothly it was discreetly kindled into the hands of millions of readers. But they cannot tell you anything about the **why**?*

Erotic literature is now openly popular as any glance at the bestseller lists will confirm. But, while we are looking for examples of our consumer's hidden life, can I ask how many of you here today or how many of your friends talk openly about buying and enjoying stories of that kind?

Quick show of hands??? Let me see . . . Ah, nobody in the entire division! Go figure!

All the Big Data in the universe cannot lever open the human heart. For the heart can truly be a very lonely hunter, sometimes harboring hard-to-discuss appetites, contrarian motives and positively sub-atomic particles of instinct and impulse—all of which can, if properly tapped, trigger but discreet credit card activity. Smart companies like ourselves constantly search for new ways to talk back to those inner voices. That is, without doubt, one of the essential purposes of our meeting today.

Let me continue. The theme is still . . .

How to be an antenna brand

For sure, Big Data can tell us of a middle-aged man's propensity to develop certain types of cancer. It can identify when a shopper's habits show telling variations and kinks—suggesting perhaps that a baby is due or that a house-move is imminent. It can optimize the drive home from work by allowing clever crowd-sourcing systems to manage traffic flows and correct bottlenecks.

However, all the digital breadcrumbs you can put on the table will still not, on their own, make an apple pie.

Life provides many daily examples of my point here.

One might well be able to log and interrogate every birthday present a man has bought for his wife for the twenty years of their marriage. For one can remotely learn much about the specific occasion in, say, June when—let's give our man a name—Jack visits an upscale store somewhere on the Bay and lays down $200 dollars or more for a single item along with the purchase of a designer birthday card.

One might well track and read significance into any shifts in his spend, the appearance of recurring preferences for certain types of gift. But can the source which reveals all this really pinpoint the most likely selection for this year, the gift that will be a definite winner? Can the source capture, from year to year, the level of satisfaction inwardly felt but not necessarily expressed by the recipient?

Can the source anticipate the reaction when Jack—true story this, as I recently learned—completely breaks with tradition this year and, thinking he is rolling in the deep of popular trends, buys his lovely wife a leather-bound volume entitled **The Very Best of Canadian Erotic Verse**?

The short answer has to be: No.

For there will surely be in play:

- *The inability of either party to be completely honest with each other.* She does not want to hurt his feelings at the moment when she unwraps this year's ribboned package. He does not really know whether the things she used to like are the same things she likes now but cannot put questions delicately enough to her in order to establish this either way.
- *The questionable value of repeat-behavior on the part of the shopper to any independent analysis.* A history of buying, say, jewelry items cannot, on its own, indicate the success that has been, in emotional reality, resulting from this kind of choice. And if Jack buys **Jean Patou Joy Eau de Parfum** for three years on the run, then the pattern is surely likely to be broken soon. But in what direction?
- *The power of whatever innovation is taking place in the evolution or the marketing of luxury.* Big Data invites nobody in the business community to stop trying to seduce customers with fresh ideas, with the chance to kick out of the box. Big Data is not some kind of armistice signaling the end of brand-to-brand warfare. Even if a famous whiskey or a designer fashion house or a big firm that makes household cleaning products . . . were to procure all the big data they could possibly find **plus** the best analytical processing systems **plus** the very best data scientists in this whole field . . . then this would not guarantee them total domination of their marketplace.

Big Data tools are being distributed around every major consumer-facing company in every sector. These tools are truly fabulous in what they can reveal, in the beautiful patterns they identify. But I have got to thinking that it is as if all the companies are being armed with exactly the same tactical nuclear weapons. As Big Data is universalized so its power is, in a sense, democratized across the marketplace. And so, it will still fall to the inspired, ingenious marketer to create new forms of differentiation for products and brands—and to do so as a result of knowing their customers better than those customers know themselves.

And so, I return to my earlier point. We must now cut out any questions or any approach to questioning which is not seriously functional. If we lose old bits of stuff, then so be it. It's a new dawn, it's a new day. We will reap real big rewards from this, both immediately and in years to come.

Charts in the key of life

So, we require a lot more imagination and flair in how we interpret the answers we receive from our customers in both quantitative and qualitative surveys. I do not want to see those customers in silhouette. I want to get to know them as multi-colored human beings. What is that line from Walt Whitman we learned at school? **I want to hear America singing!**

Take the questions we ask about what people want out of life.

Well, of course, the majority say things like: "to make other people happy and build a loving family".

Very few say: "You know what, I really need to have a better car in the driveway than that airhead next door".

Who on earth is going to tell us that their family is just not a priority in their lives? I myself have two teenage sons. You could not meet two more psychotically lazy, more dismally ungrateful wretches. If you ask them to come away from their games console because the house is on fire, they would grunt that their human rights were being violated. But, **as a Mom who knows how Moms are meant to be seen**, would I let anything of this ever creep into answers I give to a pollster? Bet your life.

We need to turn questions into cutlery. We do not want to hear nursery rhymes. We are not in an old episode of **Friends** around here. We are in a fresh episode of **CSI** every day.

When we ask simple Agree-Disagree questions, we have to thrash the meaning out of the answers.

Let me give you some examples of what I mean. I am talking about . . .

The truths that can walk only sideways

We have to check for the possibility that, in the drafting of a question, we have done little more than sharpen the invitation to respondents to agree with what they think the "normal" answer would be.

Specifically, what we must always scrutinize is the distribution between those who Agree Strongly and those who Agree Slightly—because the presence of the latter option can often act as a prompt to the lazy or the cautious or the self-aware in our midst, a chance to mask what is really felt or thought in fealty to a more socially "normal" idea.

*All opinion-research questioning is an invitation to the respondent to express his or her essential **respectability**.*

Have you ever interviewed someone, say a young graduate, for a job? During the interview, have you ever heard yourself ask something like: "What in your view has been your most significant achievement to date?". Now, has anyone in your experience ever replied with: "I got an essay off the internet—my professor failed to notice and graded me an A". Or: "I hooked up with the trainee geography teacher when I was in 12th grade and nobody knew". Next time you come across someone who lists "fluent French" as a personal skill, just say to him "J'ai de beaux yeux, n'est-ce pas?"—and note the sadly vacant stare.

*Sometimes, in surveys, people are asked how much alcohol they drink per week. I read a **Gallup** survey some time back which said that two-thirds of Americans are drinkers and the average intake was four drinks per week. Does that sound right with you? How do you think it would turn out if we made an estimate of what such figures meant for the total level of alcohol consumption in any one year and compared it with industry sales data for the same year? Would one number divided by the other equal one?*

Let's have another poll!

Hands in the air if you had more than four glasses of wine or more than four bottles of beer last week?

Come on—the truth shall set you free!

Ah, only one person. Clint, Head of Sales! Go figure again! He probably needs it.

*All the conversations we have from hour to hour, in whatever situation, do not naturally fill with pure disclosure. The power of this truth is easily and dangerously under-acknowledged by the insight functions in a company such as ours. Self-reporting of how much fruit we eat, how often we make a proper breakfast, how often we go for a run, how many times each month we cook a family meal using only fresh ingredients, how many martinis we have before Sunday lunch, how much we give to charity, how much plastic and paper we recycle from our homes, how often we call our grandma back East . . . reflects objective reality about as well as a regular episode of **True Blood** reflects the average young girl's life in 21st century small town Louisiana.*

*Nobody in the business of getting America to consume more Vitamin C would ever run a campaign on some version of: "We know (because you have told us) that you all eat tons of fresh fruit every day but see if you can squeeze down just one more orange"—**unless** the campaign managers concluded, from a range of tactical options, that flattery was the best route to victory.*

*In other words, there might well be prosperity in the idea that a Vitamin C campaign should a) check out just how much fruit people say that they consume b) assume with good reason that the figure is exaggerated by many c) act as if their target consumers want to be considered responsible, health-aware citizens who know what they ought to eat every day d) invite them into a fantasy world in which they are truly their better, more adult selves. Campaigns which promise some form of blame or implied social ostracism—**Listen up, you*** *fat Americans over there on that sofa. Stop being so trivial with your lives and eat like proper grown-ups do. And stop pretending your blueberry-flavored bubblegum is a piece of fruit!*—might also address the very measurable tendency that we all have to exaggerate our virtue and our discipline. But, the cleverest strategy, we might think, will always negotiate with both the social norm and the reality of human under-performance.

We all try to put our better selves on display—our sober, balanced, professional selves. This is why companies spend fortunes trying to perfect the best interview techniques and how they still get so many appointments horribly wrong—even as the Big Data avalanche sweeps down the mountainside.

We all try not to hurt feelings, specially our own feelings of pride and status. We all try to keep our own opinions at least slightly muted or obliquely expressed in situations where we think that too much overt truthfulness might do damage, however slight, to our personal reputational assets. You bump into an old friend in the street. You have not seen him for some time. He compliments you on the way you are looking and suggests that you must be working out a lot. Do you disillusion him? Do you say: **No, I never really bother with that sort of thing**—even though you damn well do a great deal?

Imagine that you cannot stand your boss and are annually asked to give feedback on her leadership skills to a manager from HR. How far is it wise to go, how incisive should your language be?

And if your husband leaves you, do you really want to hear by just how much, department by intimacy department, you came up short? You say you do but . . .

We all make judgements like this, employ little deceptions, enact lies of omission, face only what we want to face, nudge the conversation towards the space where we are most confident.

Let's move down into this story as it affects our way of thinking.

Imagine that 80% of people in the Mid West agree that they do indeed always try to buy home-grown American produce when they visit the grocery store.

Then imagine two circumstances—one in which 10% agree strongly and 70% agree slightly and another in which 40% agree strongly and 40% agree slightly. Would make you think, no? The total is still 80% but the meaning and the consequence for those outlets trying to maximize their grocery sales in Kansas is not likely to be the same in both instances.

Indeed something might well be assumed about the actual intensity of feeling in each case. Quite possibly, the intensity could be explored further in any experiment in which a price premium is put on products which blatantly bore Uncle Sam's image. Perhaps we could examine whether the impulse to patriotic purchasing varies across product categories. Then we would need to develop some sense of where any such impulse is, culturally and politically, headed in the future so that we can begin to plan to take advantage of it inside our brand development. In such an endeavor, the goal is to so slice public opinion that we end up knowing what customers want us to think about them—and act accordingly.

But let's get back to our style of questioning and interpreting. Imagine asking six questions, not together, one each in separate surveys, taken into the field at different times in an omnibus. They are all Agree-Disagree statements. If you now open the dossier I have had placed in front of each of you, you will discover that they are:-

- The first duty of big American companies is to make profits for their shareholders.
- The first duty of big American companies is to produce more jobs so that American families can prosper.
- The first duty of big American companies is to provide health insurance to their employees.

- The first duty of big American companies is to engage with the community in the places where they operate and invest in good works there.
- The first duty of big American companies is to keep prices as low as possible for American consumers like myself.
- The first duty of big American companies is to pay all their taxes in full and on the date due.

As you read the statements, consider the nature of the invitation to what I will call cultural conformism that is carried in each—but not always to the same extent. Some are bound to attract more clear affirmations of support (Agree Strongly) than others. Can we imagine that many Americans will be moderately supportive of each? Well, yes, we might.

*Now, as we sit round now and start guessing how respondents would react to the statements, let's ask ourselves what would happen and **what might change** under the following circumstances? Again, see the page in your dossier.*

a) *The statements are all put together as they are on the page in front of you and the sample is asked to respond to each, one after the other*

b) *The statements are presented to a selection of Moms and Dads as they leave the supermarket, having just spent $150 on all the meals and drinks and toiletries for the family—in other words, the weekly shop*

c) *The statements are put to our representative sample of Americans in a specially organized phone interview in their homes during Thanksgiving*

d) *The statements are raised at focus groups engaging blue-collar workers in Ohio, high-tech entrepreneurs in California, organic farmers from the Mid-West, business school graduands . . .*

e) The statements are put into a questionnaire which makes it clear that the market research is being carried out in our own corporate name

f) The statements are put to our representative sample immediately after a significant shock or disaster: a huge oil slick in the Gulf of Mexico, a terrible drought in the Mid West, a new corruption scandal on Wall Street, the sudden inundation of entire States

It is not good enough merely to acknowledge that the circumstance of the questioning may well alter responses. It is our job to search for truths as irreducible as they can be—using all our wits and devices in the midst of such complexity. How much of our customers' opinions is bendable, contingent, moderate rather than either intense or shallow? And when does an answer change or only seem to change because of the circumstances in which it is asked? This is what we need to establish.

*Now, the image of big companies—companies like ours—in American society references a debate that is political, cultural, social and—you will know what I mean—**inner**.*

When our Board discusses such issues as our online corporate identity, our human resources philosophy, our philanthropic and charitable programs, the search for competitive differentiation against other corporate players in our field . . . then its members have every right to expect that their in-house insight people, those who give them advice, will have learned important skills by now, skills which can help identify the costs and the advantages attending all policy choices.

I am talking about how to feel the vibrations of public opinion, screening out the ultimately insignificant tremors, recognizing the many things that will be voiced in company but not thought (perhaps even rejected) in private, thus knowing what to ignore. You can do this only by approaching both people and subjects from different angles, asking the same basic questions in slightly different ways, positively inviting uncertainties and contradictions, pruning hearsay evidence.

Are there folks out there who really do not care what big companies do for as long as their own jobs are secure and prices are low in the shops? Yes, there are. Are there folks who hate the guts of corporate America? Yes, there are. Our job is to identify how many are really in each category, no matter what they say out loud. And what really lies—in every sense of the word—in between.

I am talking about the troubling reality that . . .

The consumer has the right (and quite often the unrecognized desire) to remain silent

In stories like these, we also have to keep listening to what I call the **NANDO** *faction.*

Too often, we track only levels of agreement in our survey work. But, issue by issue, we should also follow those who do not seem to have an emphatic view, those who Neither Agree Nor Disagree. We should do this in order to see where and when this constituency is a) numerically significant or b) shifting over time—and in order to perhaps see the shadow which such a stance throws over all the whole concept of **agreement** *with whatever proposition is being put to people. In other words, our analysis query becomes: are the lines between the formal responses—Agree Strongly to Disagree Strongly—often not really distinct borders and clear delineations at all? Is it possible that what we see in the print-out is a distribution of socialized responses, mixed with a small pulse of really emphatic views, in favor or against?*

I'll give you an example. I notice that, as reported by one of our trends agencies, around 60% of Americans "wish big companies were more prepared to apologize in public when things go wrong". As a signal to corporations like ours, that seems pretty unambiguous. It surely sends a strong message to our after-sales people, to those who coach our in-store assistants, to those in our midst who have just presided over failed product launches, to those who handle our public relations from state to state. It suggests contrition in the light of under-performance is not just good for the soul but potentially very positive for customer relations.

But how should we interpret the strangely mute presence—the 30% of Americans who are the NANDOs here? Is that figure of 30% actually big enough to suggest that **most** of America is much less interested in how, in this sense, polite are the companies which sell them things every day. Corporate America might be induced into believing that it needs a shot at redemption every now and then. The individual American, for his or her part, might actually rather have a shot of bourbon at the end of a hard day's work than fretting too much about breast-beating CEOs on **CNN** or **Fox.**

Now, you people here might think it obvious and natural that ordinary folks always want to see power taken down a peg. Of course, there is a widespread feeling that big companies can be too voracious in their pursuit of profit and often cut corners or engage in sharp practice. And yes, it is a social and cultural construction that American audiences love any invitation both to scold and to forgive. If you think I make too much of this, then try watching the mid-morning programs on TV.

More, if we start to suspect that the 60% figure represents an exaggeration of what our citizens really care about, then our work is still ahead of us. By reference to what other intelligence or assumption, could we correct that figure—somehow make it more real? How many of the 60% would really spill over into the NANDO category—if we referenced into the analysis, say, their concerns about prices in the shops or their worries for their kids' futures or their response to crime levels in their neighborhoods and thus give the story a kind of **emotional scale**?

It is not that we are cynics. It's just that we have to find ways of isolating the social conversation underpinning this kind of public debate.

We should never assume that it is only the voices we hear loud and clear—the voices that like to **affirm**—that are invariably the most important, the most informative voices in the room.

Ask a silly question and you may still get a useful reply

It may also be the case that the intuition we draw from some research findings is that the people interviewed are being **too** opinionated.

Take those studies in which people are asked which is the brand they trust most, the brand of—let's select—insurance company or family car or skin care . . .

I read somewhere recently that in Germany the top answers are respectively **Allianz, Volkswagen** and **Nivea**.

Is there any quality of revelation at all in such a set of answers?

Is insight really being enriched in any way by this discovery?

If I had given all of you a couple of hours in which to do some online research and predict which brands Germans might well pick in each category then many of you would most assuredly have named . . . **Allianz, Volkswagen** and **Nivea**. Each is an enormously potent, nationally immersive brand in Germany; name recognition is pretty well absolute. And they are German-born brands with substantial market share.

This being so, it is not at all clear that the objective level of trust in such brands is what is actually being measured in such research. These are selections which it is psychologically easy and somehow reassuringly safe for consumer-citizens to make. These are brands which have built a powerful psychic resonance in German life. Choosing them is like going to the same church every Sunday or taking the same route to the office every morning or singing the national anthem at a football game. Yes, of course, many consumers will have had positive experience of the brand's products and performances and will want, in response to a survey request, to show goodwill towards it. But the exam is too easy. For such an exercise on its own tells us precious little about the strengths and vulnerabilities inhabiting the market performance of each brand.

Now, I am happy to guess that the leaderships of these three brands are not stupid people. They will be able to separate real currency from fool's gold amid the dialogue with their consumers. But oh, how beguiling the trite praise of the under-interrogated consumer can be to brand managers everywhere. This will not be our downfall here.

What do I think a high level of expressed trust in a set of consumer brands such as ours might practically indicate?

Well, *I* think it tells us something about how much experimentation our customers will tolerate from us, how much innovation—for which they have previously expressed no particular desire—they will accept. Trust, in other words, can be seen as a form of exploitable impassivity on the part of our shoppers, born of a name recognition built over years and a general sense that we are unlikely to do anything which might damage our good repute.

If you visit a branch of **McDonald's** in Spokane or, for that matter, in Stuttgart then you might be content, on a particular day, to take the invitation to switch out of your usual Big Mac to a sandwich from the company's newly launched but temporary Tex-Mex range. But if your regular hot dog stand on Main Street introduces a new spicy mutton filling from an old Ugandan recipe then you may well be less motivated to taste and try.

Not for the first time, the discussion turns on this. When consumers tell us something, which question are they actually answering?

The second hand unwinds, time after time

Finally, think about this with me.

When we ask people to report on how much time-pressure there is in their lives we always find a steady majority who say that those pressures are daily and serious. And, of course, so much product innovation in so many sectors has over the years addressed this human story in very direct and productive ways: everything from pressure cookers to shampoo-and-conditioner sets to executive car washes. The internet, of course, is the greatest time-saving product of all. Who can imagine a time when we all had to visit a bookstore to buy a novel or run our own garage sale to get rid of old children's clothes or movies?

But the striking thing is that the time-sequence data here will not show a decrease in the number of people saying that they have trouble cramming into each day all that they want or need to do. Now, of course, severe time-pressure must be real enough in many a life. A single Mom who runs two low paid jobs, while working downtown but living outside the city limits, will unquestionably have her strife. And many in this room will know what it is like for a woman who does well in her career but still has to shoulder all the home-building and child-care duties.

But in our culture few of us will want to call attention to the fact that we have time on our hands or are just not bothering to build any personal achievements these days. America loves busy people.

*So, my question becomes. What is the true commercial dynamic in this story now? What does a company like ours **notice** about it?*

*Is it possible that there are brands out there today which a) have noted that folks like to affirm that they are under time-pressure b) have invented products which promise that, by their use, time will be saved c) bring such products to market while knowing or anticipating that they will beckon consumers **to spend more time using them*** *rather than less and that this will be to those consumers' actual benefit?*

Consider those high-tech booths you see nowadays in upscale department stores—the ones which take your size digitally when you go to buy a pair of pants. The promise is a faster route to jeans that will fit really well—an experience both practically satisfying and time-saving. But, of course, a digital sizing booth is fun; its processes make everyone and everyone's body shape interesting. It will generate all kinds of options and ideas from a wide range of designers—styles, colors, cuts, prices . . . My guess is that the convenience proposition here will soon give way to a pretty premium shopping experience in which the customer becomes ever more engaged. No deceit is practiced. There is no sleight of hand. But the initial questioning of consumers about an important source of pressure in their lives is well used, well **weighed**. Think too of those cookbooks which tell you that, if you follow the instructions from the celebrity chef, a tasty and nutritious family meal will follow in 15 minutes. But the fun and the challenge of cooking the meal might well soon and silently overwhelm the desire to create good fast food. Maybe no-one will really notice that tonight's dinner took, in fact, 27 minutes to prepare. The people who might well have told researchers that they never have time to cook properly will be the very same people who like and enjoy a product which, in the end, speaks but superficially to their I-am-a-very-busy-person ethic.

Let's take a break now. But let me summarize. What is it that we are inviting ourselves to address?

- **Whereas all answers to opinion research questions will be valuable to some extent, we must in the interest of our brand's health ask only excellent, only really incisive questions.**
- **When our customers speak to us, there is a filter of social conventions and expectations wrapped around their answers. Our job is to find the irreducible truths in what they are saying while recognizing that those conventions and expectations are sensitive matters to people. They will**

not want them to be ignored or minimized or parodied. But they will not necessarily want them to be taken or treated literally.

- *All our opinion research findings must feed discrete socio-cultural trends. We have to capture human behavior and its capacity for change in envelopes of flexible thought and prediction. If our trends carry no predictive power, then they are defective and are probably draining serious energy from the quality of our strategy.*

- *Understanding the reason for any human exaggeration, any unwillingness to admit to a feeling or an opinion, any downright big lie . . . is the skill which can increase our marketplace strength. We are going to get really good at it . . .*

So let's reconvene in an hour. There are consequences for the way we do things around here in everything I have been saying.

Lisa will take us through them . . .

POSTSCRIPT

This book is the outcrop of countless debates and arguments among Future Foundation staffers and, in turn, with clients and collaborators in all business sectors, from the USA and Europe.

Any and all of the book's vices are the work of the authors themselves. All of the virtues, such as they might be, are the fruit of a huge co-operative effort mounted inside the company and stretching back down the years.

Since Future Foundation's birth, the big questions we have been asked to address all come down to some pretty simple ones. Such as: *Thanks for your charts, now so what? How does this knowledge really help drive our business to a more secure and profitable state? We are not interested in just facts-and-figures or interesting commentaries on consumer behavior—so which trends present real opportunities for a company like ours?*

Alongside our trends-creation and trends-monitoring activities across the world, the **Big Lie** evolved in part as an answer to such interrogation. We set out to make our story here true and compelling and valuable. Our readers and our clients will decide if it hits those targets.

This seems like a good moment to thank our Chair, Melanie Howard, who has been such an energizing presence behind this whole venture. We must also thank our fellow board directors Deborah Parkes and Colin Lloyd for their constant encouragement and ever constructive comments.

And to the multi-lingual, multi-cultural and multi-talented staff at our HQ, we also express our serious gratitude. A group of more—in the best possible way—argumentative people you could not want to meet. We would not have it any other way.

We have a company rule. Any member of staff and any client of whatever rank can speak directly to the Future Foundation CEO about any subject at any time. It is simply a question of getting on the phone or starting an email.

And so, if you have any comments about our **Big Lie** analysis, want to challenge anything we say here or would simply like to continue the discussion about the themes we raise, then you can get me here anytime.

christophej@futurefoundation.net / + 44 (0)20 3008 4889

Or, if you prefer, you can reach us on twitter.com/futurethoughts or linkedin.com/company/future-foundation—and start a dialogue that way. We have also created a special website thebigliebook.net. Check us out.

Thank you for taking a copy of our book. We hope it stimulates you. We hope it helps you in your business decisions. Perhaps it has made you think differently and in a good way.

Warmest regards,

Christophe Jouan

September 2013

GLOSSARY OF
FUTURE FOUNDATION TRENDS

Our trends are envelopes of observation, reflection and prediction.

They are coined by our globally recruited specialist team in the light of our proprietary opinion research findings, our tracking of market innovations and business start-ups, our ingesting of new books and propositions about social change, our interpretation of macro-economic forecasts, our awareness of the politics prevailing in the era we inhabit and the one we are about to enter. The trends are all captured inside our syndicated service **nVision**.

They are often the offspring of the structural and the discretionary forces in all our lives.

By **structural**, we address the things which no individual can directly or immediately change: the country of his/her birth, the demographics of the age, the general state of the economy and the buying power of families, the climate, the condition of the environment, the doings of the party in power . . .

By **discretionary**, we address the choices that individuals can be considered generally free to make: where to live, whom to marry, with what to furnish the home, what books and magazines and TV shows to read/watch, how to dress each morning, whether to drink wine or beer or cola, which church (if any) to attend . . .

Across our **nVision US**, **nVision EU** and **nVision Global** services we run approximately 100 trends, all constantly updated and renewed or, as intellectual discipline demands, shed for being no longer relevant or explanatory. We use them in our work with clients . . .

- To enrich insight and test the prospects for new product and service ideas
- To inspire new thinking about how to talk to customers in an ever more intimate tone
- To disrupt naivety, cliché, derelict assumptions— wherever such things are undermining clear strategic thinking about the future

Below is a short definition of those trends of ours which have been referenced once or more in the **Big Lie**.

Ageless Society (Chapter Two: Power of Me, Value of We)

Age-inclusive marketing communications grow in validity as a) demographic change increases the population of over-65s in many places b) millions lead longer, healthier, ever active lives while having accumulated significant spending power and c) silver role-models (movie stars, politicians, business leaders . . .) glamorize the third age and beyond.

Cheap Treats (Chapter One: Ever Smarter Consumers, Endlessly Irrational Choices)

> In a time when real incomes grow only slowly (if at all) and price sensitivity remains acute, concepts such as luxury and indulgence are easily re-defined. The appetite for premium quality can switch to lower-ticket items (cheaper wines, candy, fashions, family leisure trips . . .) and move across into completely separate categories (eg giving the expensive chocolate as a gift rather than the more expensive champagne). This is an invitation to creative re-positioning of product at all price points.

Cult of Celebrity (Chapter Three: Comfortable Lives, Uncomfortable Truths)

> It remains as true as ever that *celebrity* endorsement shifts inventory. No deceleration of this trend is detectable even as consumers grow notionally smarter and more sophisticated. Indeed, the number of product categories which can be profitably invaded by the cult of celebrity seems totally elastic (fragrances, movies, alcoholic drinks, designer wear, health foods . . .). Most global celebrities, we note, are Western while much celebrity has but a local range and value.

Cult of Home (Chapter One: Ever Smarter Consumers, Endlessly Irrational Choices)

> The home remains a cocoon. But now even an individual room can be a complete personal entertainment complex, a work station, the venue for multiple conversations with the outside world, a place to display one's taste and one's general *savoir-vivre* . . . The home is indeed multiple mini-homes and endless individualisms. This evolution naturally stimulates innovation within and competition amongst out-of-home offers—restaurants, cinemas, stadiums—as

suppliers seek to produce those experiences which simply cannot be re-produced by or for one family at home.

Culture of Fear (Chapter Four: The Call of Yesterday, the Scream of the New)

> Although statistics may well confirm that we live in a society which is cleaner, safer, healthier and better educated than ever before, many consumer-citizens remain generally suspicious and vulnerable to (oftentimes exaggerated) fears about the dangers they might encounter in their daily lives. This fuels the need for constant reassurance— from policy-makers and corporations alike. There is hardly a market left un-affected by this trend.

Everyday Exceptional (Chapter One: Ever Smarter Consumers, Endlessly Irrational Choices)

> In austere times, the search for excuses for legitimized fun or party-giving naturally accelerates. In multi-cultural societies, the number of shareable festivals and happenings seems to increase. Every day can, somewhere and somehow, be a special day—a notion which invites a wave of ever-refreshed innovations at the level of product and promotion in sectors such as foodstuffs, beverages, leisure, venues . . . All fun can be given an ever more sophisticated cultural pretext.

End of Inefficiency (The Big Lie: Using the story to push your business forward)

> It is possible that many consumers will be happy to compress their own discretion and choice-making in order to achieve better outcomes for themselves. Where there is a service which can perfect the best selection (of home utility tariff, savings account, hotel in a strange city . . .) without the consumer actually scrutinizing the

options or even effecting the switch from a previous preference . . . then there will be a market for such a service. In a practical reality as well as a metaphor, many will take the option not to drive on the freeway but have their cars driven for them by remote control.

Digital Revolution *(passim)*

No aspect of human life is left untouched by the individual's ability to communicate to audiences large and tiny across cyber-space. No opinion needs to go unvoiced. No personal interest need fail to be pursued, no experience unshared, no incident unrecorded. At the same time, a digital trail is left and vast amounts of data (our movements, our purchases, our preferences . . .) can be stored and exploited.

Healthy Hedonism (Chapter One: Ever Smarter Consumers, Endlessly Irrational Choices)

There is a natural tension between the consumer's appetite for indulgence and the invitation made (by public authorities, campaign groups, family members . . .) to that same consumer to stay healthy through personal action. This tension expresses itself in the food & drink sectors where product innovation often offers luxurious tastes combined with serious health-enhancing properties. More generally, the trend references the principle that in many markets now the promise of a treat has to be compensated by the availability of a lite or decaf option. In the basement of the deluxe hotel, there will be a rowing machine (whether used or not).

Ish! (Chapter One: Ever Smarter Consumers, Endlessly Irrational Choices)

Inter-human commitment is often becoming seasonally-renewable, performance-conditional, de-formalised, monogam-*ish*. This expresses itself in everything from rates of divorce and cohabitation, dating behavior, reality TV shows, social media activity . . . Also, this metaphors the short-termism that has crept into market relationships: few consumers want to be locked into hard-to-escape contracts or build anything other than entirely transactional and instrumentalist connections with suppliers. Whether a socially desirable phenomenon or not, nothing is for life any more.

Myth of Decline (Chapter Four: The Call of Yesterday, the Scream of the New)

Many people are easily invaded by the conviction that yesteryear was somehow a happier, safer, more benign and altogether better place to live. The notion that *nothing-is-as-good-as-it-used-to-be* represents a very potent and widespread social conversation. It will sometimes prove difficult to persuade people, even with stark evidence, that things in whatever theater of life have improved. This being so, brands which can claim a heritage and a longevity may well enjoy a privileged route into the emotions of consumer-citizens.

Native Marketing (Chapter One: Power of Me, Value of We)

As any glance at modern social media will confirm, adroit brands everywhere are becoming story-tellers and entertainment-curators—building fun narratives (games, competitions, conversation-brokering . . .) for their clubs of customers and supporters to follow. So much online marketing now takes the relationship with consumers as far away from any cold, objective discussion about price and value-for-money as it could possibly go.

Personalization of Authority (Chapter Two: Power of Me, Value of We)

It would be a well-trod assumption that the formal voices of authority in our lives are not as powerful as they used to be. Some talk of the death of deference. At the same time, millions can access multiple and independent sources of intelligence and advice (which way to vote, what to buy, which car/resort/cell phone/neighborhood/TV show to favor . . .). As individuals become more educated and more skilled, so they require less external validation of their choices in life. There are no bossy, know-it-all brands any more.

Pop Radical (Chapter Three: Comfortable Lives, Uncomfortable Truths)

> Our culture seems naturally to produce invitations to express dissatisfaction, to make complaint, even to voice outrage. Much is made of the consumer's power not just to withdraw support from a company or a brand but also of her power to lobby against or to boycott them. The internet is full of angry and disappointed people who will not let things go. But perhaps the consumer's inner clamoring can be exaggerated. For really few drift towards extreme positions or actions and sustain them. Radical attitudes transfer into radical behaviors in but limited ways. However, brands might well choose to respect those attitudes for what they reveal about how the consumers concerned like to be seen and addressed.

Vogue-Alization (The Big Lie: Using the story to push your business forward)

> Fashion is now a force for accelerated cultural colonization and consumer convergence. Its ever-evolving definition of what is beautiful and glamorous spreads Western cultural norms/values and thus seriously influences the path of globalization. The sheer desirability of European and American designer-wear in such markets as China and India would seem to confirm the story. Some expect that eventually regional/local styles and images will push back those now in favor in the worldwide fashion trades. But this is unlikely to occur soon.

THE AUTHORS

Christophe Jouan is the CEO of Future Foundation. With a personal background in sociology, math and IT, he joined the company in 1998. Having sifted many waves of quantitative research findings over this time, he has developed and applied his own personal vision of how trends analysis should  deliver quality insights on a genuinely global basis. His skill and his goal is to pioneer unique statistical analysis techniques which are versatile enough to turn raw data into liquid insight.

 **Meabh Quoirin is the MD of Future Foundation**. She oversees the company's relations with all corporate clients, anticipating and servicing their demand for usable forecasts, focused counsel, enhanced decision-taking. She delivers the Trends Keynote address at all major Future Foundation conferences. As MD of our principal syndicated service **nVision**, she runs the company's operations in both New York and London.

James Murphy is the Editorial Director of Future Foundation. His team processes all the quantitative and qualitative intelligence which the company commissions from around the world. Their job is to locate the most dynamic trends in the economy, in our culture, in society at large—and put them to work for clients.

CPSIA information can be obtained at www.ICGtesting.com
Printed in the USA
BVOW02s1153300813

329934BV00001B/1/P